# DESTINATION
# ENGAGE

Published by Engage Solutions
Group

First published in the United
Kingdom in 2022
ISBN: 9798437663325

Edited by Sarah Levick
Cartoons by Dink

Typeset and printed by
www.beamreachuk.co.uk

# DESTINATION
# ENGAGE

How three Mr Men reinvented engagement and
**made it big in the boardroom**

Phil Wedgwood

# Contents

"...interdisciplinary thinking and a **relentlessly experimental frame of mind**..."

"... a combination of business **acumen and global mindset**..."

"Wedgwood was a virtuoso businessman who combined technical **proficiency with a gifted eye for trends**..."

Financial Times
**December 2021**

JOSIAH WEDGWOOD,
FOUNDING FATHER,
INDUSTRIAL REVOLUTION

Phil Wedgwood,
contributing son,
Digital Revolution

dink

If only they'd been talking about me! Sadly for my ego the subject of this glowing profile was the rather more famous Josiah Wedgwood, "the father of English potters", and one of the founding fathers of the first Industrial Revolution. But I'm rather hoping that a fragment of that "witty, skilful, learned" DNA found its way down through the family generations as I sit here doing my bit for the digital revolution. Okay, so Great-Great-plus-a-few-more-greats Uncle Josiah may have helped change the modern world (no pressure there then!) but I'm happy to be making my small but perfectly formed contribution, leaving my own tiny footnote on the Wedgwood family tree. As that features Charles Darwin, Ralph Vaughan Williams and numerous assorted luminaries, I'll be lucky if there's room for me to scribble my initials.

Talking of scribbling...Cards on the table time. When I said I was going to write a book, I got a few raised eyebrows. Yes, I'm a business technologist and digital devotee - but I'm not Steve Jobs from the Valley, I'm Phil from Manchester. Why would anyone be interested in what I have to say?

I don't suppose I'll be troubling the Amazon bestsellers list anytime ever, but of course that was never my intention in the first place. The reason I do offer in mitigation of what might seem like an indulgent exercise is that I am truly passionate about what we have achieved here at Engage Solutions Group: not so much the growing of a successful digital business but how we've changed organisational thinking around engagement.

Engagement now has a claim to be part of the digital transformation conversation. From its colleague app beginnings to its enterprise platform maturity, it has earned its seat at the boardroom table. I wanted to dive into the how and why.

And while I have taken on story-telling duties and made my own contribution to what you're about to read, please have no doubt that this is a team effort. What we have done together is unique. No-one has evolved as we have to be able to do what we do today: helping maximise engagement and experience for the three most important audiences a business has - its colleagues, customers and wider communities.

A book gives me permission to tell that story in full, and to share the stories behind the story; to build a much better understanding of engagement and paint a bolder picture; to help everyone see its power and potential more clearly; and to get excited and enthused by the whole notion of engagement success and the 'art of the possible'.

It's been an amazing ride so far. Please join me as I relive the journey.

**Phil Wedgwood**
Engage CEO, nerdy kid turned passionate technologist, digital entrepreneur and try-hard cyclist

Manchester
Spring 2022

**DESTINATION ENGAGE**

## CHAPTER 1

Oh dear. Was the day about to go horribly wrong? I could see the CEO wasn't quite comfortable with this. The studio lights weren't helping but there was a general awkwardness in front of camera. Was he just worried about his dignity? I could sense a slight tension in the room where five minutes earlier it had been all giggles as the CMO gave a theatrical finish to her two-minute cameo to camera and curtsied her way off stage. She had been preceded by the COO, CIO and HRD, who had each given it their all, with the inevitably line fluffing met with good-natured laughter and heckling from their colleagues.

But now the CEO had stepped up, and the atmosphere seemed a tad strained. He was cued in by our studio manager, he looked straight at the autocue, opened his mouth to speak and promptly stumbled over his name. A second's embarrassed pause, then a bit of classical Anglo-Saxon four-letter vernacular and a painful hush. Then, suddenly, the COO absolutely erupted, creasing with laughter. Which, of course, set off the inevitable chain reaction, as cracking up when you really shouldn't is just one of those unavoidable social solecisms and physical impossibilities. I could feel myself on the cusp of the point-of-no-return, the pressure building in my chest, my face contorting under the strain of suppressing an unseemly outburst: if I started I wouldn't be able to stop and how would that look?

I fixed my gaze on the CEO – I couldn't decide whether he was going to sack everyone on the spot or leave in high dudgeon. As the orchestrator of this whole occasion, I felt I should do or say something but before I could pre-empt a possible 'situation' there was a loud guffaw from the stage and the CEO totally lost it. He was a big man and when he laughed, you didn't just hear it, you felt it too. Of course, that set everyone off again and with the tension suddenly evaporating, I called a timeout and shepherded everyone to the green room for some refreshment.

An hour later, with the CEO's five-minute speech safely in the can with only a small smattering of swear words to be edited out, we were out of the studio, and with the work done, it was time to hit the drinks fridge and kick back. As the CEO and I chinked beer bottles, he nodded and said "Phil, it's been brilliant". I would have welled up with happiness if I hadn't already filled up with relief. I had been so desperate for things to go well, to see if we could turn the vision that I had had in my head for so long into a reality. In that three-word verdict I had my answer.

So what was that vision and what was this reality? That's what I'm about to explore in Destination Engage.

Yes, I know what you're thinking, Destination Engage sounds like an end point, and a bit of weird opener for a book – weren't we always told to start at the beginning?

Well, I've never been one to follow convention so we're starting at the end – trust me, it will all make sense.

Destination Engage inspired the book title. It started life in my head and came to life with the above C team and their burgeoning blooper reel. It was the first ever 'Destination Engage' event: a specially curated two-day session for a large manufacturer that my company – Engage Solutions Group – put together to help Company X develop a whole new engagement strategy.

I remember everything about that day so, so clearly. By the time we'd gone down into our studio (specifically to demonstrate some of the augmented reality capability we'd been developing – but also just lighten the tenor of the day and have some team-building fun while we were at it), the five-strong exec team and my team had already clocked up three intensive sessions of strategy, planning and business case development. They'd also enjoyed a working lunch getting up close and personal with our technology: we're rare in this space in having brandable, oven-ready apps for both internal and external engagement and so everyone duly put our colleague app, community app and customer app through their paces.

As we walked down to the studio, the COO and I fell into step and he gave me the first inkling that we had actually pulled this off. He told me how excited everyone was, how galvanised they'd been by the approach we'd taken. Even the prospect of getting on stage and talking to camera – out of the comfort zone for all of them – was eagerly anticipated as the whole vibe was so positive, everyone felt relaxed, and they just wanted to get up there and give it a go. Yes, it was a bit left field but in a world of corporate blandness sometimes left field is the right call. And in my eyes, Destination Engage was more than just an event, it also represented the final stage of the ESG journey: the distillation of everything we knew about engagement, the culmination of both our thinking and our technology, and the creative sharing of that knowledge with others.

This was where we knew we wanted to get to, this chance to redefine engagement entirely, to transform how others saw it – and to put it at the very heart of a modern business.

**In the beginning**
At the start of our journey back in late 2017, engagement was defined very narrowly. It was an HR and employee 'thing', and it even had its own Gartner category - employee engagement.  It was based on the annual engagement score organistions monitored, and our early conversations were skewed very much towards surveys and rewards and benefits. When you think about it properly, with all the complex dynamics of a workforce and the psychology of its human components to factor in, how far could such limited activities push that employee engagement needle? How do those things improve experience, drive commitment, enhance performance, get staff to a happiness or satisfaction level that triggers that all-important discretionary effort? The answer is, they don't. Not in isolation, not without other factors in

play, not without a proper strategic framework to be able to pull all the requisite 'agents of change' together and deliver them directly to every individual on staff.

We set ourselves the task of building that proper framework and the technology to bring it to life – designing and delivering a new take on employee/colleague engagement that culminated in what has since become a class-leading workforce app. It has encouraged companies to completely reframe how they see engagement, moving beyond the perks and the paper mountain that characterised most annual staff check-ins; now it's about connections and conversations, collaboration and culture; empowering and enabling and encouraging the employee, while returning efficiency, compliance, quality and performance gains to the employer. It's about tackling staff churn and workplace stress and low productivity, eliminating the waste of human capital, and instead investing people with purpose, the better to power profit and growth.

We also rode a wave – or even powered it in some cases perhaps. The last decade has seen a radical acceleration in digitalisation, with, for once, the consumer market leading the way. There was a time when the technology you enjoyed at work far outstripped what you were likely to have at home. First Microsoft and then Apple turned that equation on its head, with the iPhone putting unprecedented power in the pocket of individuals and Big Tech following in its wake with a whole new transformational world of apps and social platforms.

It's little wonder that you have phenomena like shadow IT causing CIOs so much angst. Unsanctioned apps in use for company work? Files getting pinged right, left and centre via cloud transfer tools without any security or data privacy controls? Messaging tools in daily use outside of the corporate firewall in strict contravention of

GDPR? But it's happening because the tools are clever, quick, easy to access and so proficient at doing the one job they're being asked to do – and because the corporate IT team haven't delivered anything of comparable quality. Nature abhors a vacuum – so do employees, which is why they get creative and go and find their own funky, user-friendly solutions.

Having spent a decade in the legal technology market it's one I'm familiar with and still keep tabs on. I find it hard to fathom why even now, in the early '20s, I can see fee earner tools that look like they were built in the nineties, with a strong anachronistic whiff of Visual Basic and Microsoft Access. Have they not noticed there's been a web revolution? Followed by an app revolution? I appreciate that there's a high degree of complexity going on behind the scenes but apart from some visual dashboarding it's akin to the BBC not realising it can broadcast in colour.

So here we all are away from work, surfing on our sofas, streaming on the beach, Whatsapping our mates, scrolling through our feeds, clicking on that weird looking melon that Ocado has popped up in your suggestions. While here in work...it's all a bit dull. Except when we're Whatsapping our colleagues, which may well be in contravention of every data protection policy going but what else do we have?

It was that 'disconnect' between work and play that gave the Engage team the first of our 'if we could just' moments. If we could just harness some of the slickness and intuitiveness in social media platforms, or in the news or shopping apps that has allowed everyone, from 8 to 80, to just pick up their smartphone and swipe, tap and type with zero instruction, it would be huge. Because the framework we'd been playing with – trying to really nail down the core engagement pillars that you would stand up in your business and then build around, replacing all of those siloed 'point solutions' - that framework would only come alive if we also draped around it an electric user experience. The sort of easy, dynamic, interactive, and enjoyable experience we were now having every day: in short, the sort of experience that people were now expecting.

Before we set about spending seven figure sums in R&D we wanted to be sure we fully understood the problem we were going to be solving. Even though engagement practices seemed well established in HR management we found few vendors or HR teams that could easily define it. I wasn't seeing many company engagement strategies, nor much of a take on what success would look like, and certainly no framework to guide the journey to success. We kept running into annual surveys masquerading as a 'strategy' – yet to us the concept felt dated and the execution was way too time-consuming. Our default position even back then was that we wanted tech that just tapped into the engagement vibe of a business, connecting into the workforce to measure the heartbeat in real-time. We've been an instant, real-time world for a while now - you shouldn't be surveying people once a year to know about employee experience and satisfaction.

The R&D phase took months and millions; we consulted widely with executive teams both here in the UK and US, and had inputs from the likes of Deloitte who were the earliest champions of our defining 'digital enablement and transformation' message.

Even so, I still feel that what we ultimately delivered was more than people expected: a colleague app (with the more inclusive 'colleague' preferred to 'employee') engineered around a freshly minted framework built on five 'engagement pillars': communications, accessibility, enablement, recognition, and feedback; inspired by social media to give that instant familiarity and cool look, with the Facebook-esque feed and the WhatsApp-style messaging. It was stylish and new but somehow recognisable and reassuring. But it was what the app came with that really defied initial expectations – and looking back I see that these were the seeds of an engagement project that has now reached its final destination.

For one thing, it is customary to root an app sale in a forensic business case prepared by us in collaboration with the client's C team of execs – the question 'what does success look like?' is always answered in the most impressive granular detail, not with illustrative generic returns but hard maths as it related to the prospect's business.

The deployment phase is driven by our project management team who share vast amounts of knowledge with clients in very short timeframes. How to launch successfully, how to drive positive adoption early, how to manage across myriad demographics and IT literacy levels, the tips and tricks to help 'ignite' usage, all of this is on hand from real-life, contactable, empathetic humans, not some DIY knowledge base.

Nor are our apps left unloved and unmanaged, as our customer success team resolutely stays in play after launch. Their focus? Keeping clients on track, reviewing milestones, analysing data, previewing new features, remediating particular issues, staying totally invested in the client's progress not with the app per se, but the wider engagement project with the app as the enabling engine.

It was then, and still is today, a very different way of doing things in this market. The majority of providers in the employee engagement space are pure app plays – you're buying software, not specialist help. But it's help that people want. They don't have all the answers, they can't be experts in everything, what they want more than anything else is most definitely not an app that just puts more on their plate – that app has to wrapped up in a workable strategy or a pragmatic approach that they understand and can be confident in implementing, buoyed by the external team advising them. In the beginning, we didn't ever reference it as consulting, it was just what we did naturally – we wanted clients to be successful and that meant guiding their journey, not just handing them a map and telling them to find their own way.

When you start off you are always looking for those signs that tell you that you have made the right call. Were we right to invest in so much 'heavy touch' human interaction and advisory work when everyone else was so hands-off? I think we got our answer quite early on in a little run of sales opportunities where, by chance, we crashed the party very late. Three times we were told 'you've missed the boat', three times we argued persuasively to be seen, three times we got added to the shortlist. Twice we got the final nod too, and the feedback from the clients all ran along very similar lines – that we were the first vendor who had really put engagement in a proper business context; who had developed a cogent framework that could underpin a variable speed, multi-layer programme; and who had the people to help them make a success of the app.

It was just the sort of validation we needed back then, and the tier one client wins that followed built both our commercial standing and our confidence. By early 2020, we had already established ourselves as an ever present in the Top 50 of the business App Store; our colleague engagement app was in tens of thousands of pockets across retail, manufacturing, transport, logistics, healthcare, leisure, automotive and industrial organisations. It wasn't enough though. This was just stage one, base camp. There was more to engagement than just this internal movement. I had been excited by the tools and techniques in play and how some of our clients had embraced our idea of owning the colleague journey – where the relationship is a genuine continuum, with employees supported and engaged all day in every way, and not just at the classic touch points of 'onboarding' or 'appraisal' or 'survey'.

Wouldn't that same idea translate externally, couldn't you use apps and some of these communication and transactional tools to own the customer journey too? Couldn't we start to reframe customer engagement and extend the ESG narrative to start talking about engagement in the round, internal and external? The irony here of course was that in moving organisations along their own engagement journey, so I was moving ESG along ours.

Destination Engage was one step closer.

*"YOU CAN TAKE AN ANALOGY TOO FAR, YOU KNOW"*

**PLATFORM 5C**

### CHAPTER 2

I'm conscious that in all my
excitement I've rushed you headlong
into the ESG story, mixing endings
and beginnings and hinting that
there's a story in getting from one to
the other. Now I just want to pause
and help you get your bearings
before we crack on.

02

Today, to arrive at Destination Engage, you get off at Platform 5C. In one number and one letter, there you have it: the distillation of what ESG is and does:

- Colleague engagement
- Customer engagement
- Community engagement
- Platform-enabled content
- Consultancy

"WHAT PART OF 'ANALOGY' AND 'TOO FAR' DIDN'T YOU UNDERSTAND?"

We've come a long way because we left from Platform 1C. Back in the day we were just a colleague app, running along HR and internal comms tracks. And yet here we are, 5Cs to the good! Every bit of our value and differentiation is wrapped up in that two-digit descriptor: whenever I'm in with CEOs I do my best to articulate the power and the purpose of the 5Cs and why they set us apart. It's not some flaky marketing gimmick, it's the thing that underscores our capability and reinforces our credibility. It's essentially everything you will read about in this book but if I had to summarise it then it would go something like this:

- We own the technology platform, in the form of our front-end apps and underpinning stack. That gives you your end-to-end enterprise engagement solution, which you can deploy at your own pace, pivoting from colleague to customer or community audiences when you are ready

- We have a wealth of engagement knowhow and expertise, together with real-world data analytics, to draw on to help clients on their own engagement journeys. That's not just best practice generally but also sector level smarts, knowing what works for a particular industry. This extends from account managers supporting day-to-day client contacts to Engage CXOs peering at board level and driving the strategic conversations.

- We own and operate our own production team and digital FX studio, and we champion content strategy. We have a deep understanding of the power of content and the type, blend and cadence needed for enduring engagement. We also complement standard digital content creation with our own specialisation in delivering platform-enabled output, such as augmented reality (AR) videos that use the AR functionality native in our platform.

To the best of my knowledge there is no-one else in the marketplace that has adopted this tightly bound, highly complementary 360° approach or even looked to straddle both internal and external engagement. When I had my first thoughts of extending out to customer engagement, I was amazed to find that there wasn't a natural competitor. The customer space seemed to be divvied up between CRM systems and Net Promoter Score-centric applications; customer apps seemed very basic and largely transactional. There was no hint of anyone owning the whole customer lifecycle.

But if your commitment to customers is to improve engagement success, internally or externally or both, why would you not go there? I know that having everything under one roof in one unified ecosystem makes us better – and that clients get to enjoy the fruits of that 'better': the slicker, smarter apps; the bolder, brighter content; the sharper, savvier guidance. We'd be a lesser partner if we had stopped at that first C.

Perhaps others have swerved it because it is, quite frankly, a huge undertaking. It's taken us close on five years and many millions of investment to get to this point; our team has, ironically given our big ambitions, always stayed relatively small. But it's an agile team, an intelligent team, a pragmatic team, and like a good football unit we've made steady, regular upfield surges, building from the back, channelling it through the middle and banging it in the back of the net: the first nextgen colleague app, the first engagement platform that then unlocked successive apps dedicated to customer and community audiences; content services to help clients light up their new digital channels; and finally engagement success managers and senior consultants, real human experts to reach out and advise and make success happen – a very long way from typical SaaS vendors who just throw you the DIY lifeline of an online knowledge base and anonymous support desk.

This is a people business, people! It was always one of the oddities that struck me most forcibly as we started out: for something so intrinsically about people and the human experience, there was this illogical disintermediation going on. Organisations, at vendors' behest, were rolling out employee engagement apps with zero hands-on help; it was as basic as downloading an app off the App Store and off you go, you're on your own now. I contrasted that with our default approach: discovery sessions with a prospect's C suite; building a business case collaboratively; deployment and training; on-going account management and performance measurement against milestones and the original success criteria; regular touch-ins CEO to CEO. All done diligently but dynamically and at pace, atypical of your enterprise IT project but a nod to the need for speed and momentum.

The zero-touch stuff did explain one thing though – the litany of failed employee engagement projects we encountered. We came across a lot of disenchanted HR directors, who had made best efforts and had the best intentions too, but who ultimately were undone by the challenging complexity of employee engagement and apps that promised to be a panacea – but proved woefully ineffectual without some strategic thinking, some clear structure to help frame and then drive through what needed to be done.

Many HRs we talked to in those early days told a similar story – rolling out multiple point solutions, typically something for internal comms, for rewards and incentives, and surveys; sometimes but not always piggybacking on IT's latest intranet refresh project. It rarely sounded coherent or joined up, and it was just too onerous to orchestrate everything effectively, with more stuff falling between the cracks than landing in key sweetspots.

Those stories were invaluable when it came to formulating how we were going to shake up the employee engagement app space. For a start, we knew we had to be a tech + consulting play from the off: connecting, motivating and enabling a diverse workforce, you don't just throw an app in and hope: you make the effort to understand that business, its drivers and dynamics, and how we, together, can best leverage the technology we're going to make available to them. We had to bake that thinking into our DNA from the get-go.

Let's make that story our first stop.

**FIRST STOP**

### CHAPTER 3

A journey is a familiar metaphor for an evolution. As I look back on the past four years, I see how far we've come and can remember many of the key stops and stages en route. In business as in life you take all that wisdom and experience, the hits and misses, the wins and successes, to steer your next steps and shape future success.

But you never forget your beginnings. And the company we are today, the CEO I am today, the engagement value we offer today, owes everything to those formative months back in late 2017.

So settle down and let me tell you the story of how it all began. I could go all fancy and do one of those time jump scripts so beloved of Netflix dramas but I'd probably confuse myself so here's the potted synopsis instead. Besides you already know how this ends!

Two friends with entrepreneurial tech backgrounds looking for a new opportunity (Cast: Phil Wedgwood, Phil Ashworth)

A guy passionate about human behaviour and psychology who has co-developed the first ever employee engagement app looking for further backing (Cast: John Porter)

Phils meet John, Phils like John, John likes Phils, everyone thinks there's something in this engagement play and a deal is done

Team comes together to develop next-generation colleague engagement app

Clients go wild for it (*Enough of the sensationalism. Ed*)

The end (of the beginning)

Or as a good friend of mine more pithily captured it:

**"If Roger Hargreaves had been around to immortalise you, then the likes of Mr Tickle, Mr Greedy and Mr Bump would have been rubbing shoulders with Mr Digital, Mr Tech and Mr Engagement."**

*"WHERE'S MR ARTISTIC WHEN YOU NEED HIM?"*

Our meeting with John Porter was serendipitous, friend of a friend (successful businessman and cycling mate Mike Rogan), right place, right time sort of stuff. My friend and long-term business colleague Phil Ashworth and I had been working in the legal technology space. We'd done an earn-out from our previous business that had been sold to US legal tech behemoth Intapp, and after a bit of a break we just wanted to get back to it. But engagement? Seriously, I had to google it first, I didn't even know it was a 'thing'. That initial get-together though... I may have been hazy on the subject but I was very clear about one thing by the end of it. Correction, two things. I had just met my Mr Man, Mr Engagement. And I wanted to back him.

**John's story**

Forgive me the slight deviation here but John's story is so bound up with our story that it needs its place right here. John Porter was around engagement before it was even engagement. In the analogue era it was internal comms, all newsletters and magazines, and John helped many companies in the north-west with their print and production requirements. As digital took off, so did electronic media and the concept of the corporate intranet. John had a natural interest in behaviour and personal development and saw at first-hand the difference a commitment to communicate with and support a workforce could make. A born enthusiast and tireless with it, he helped his clients wherever he could. And slowly, engagement started to emerge as a recognised discipline. When the iPhone was born, it was only a matter of time before it 'app-ened'.

## MR. ENGAGEMENT

John understood it better than anyone and he brought to market the UK's first ever employee engagement app. It was an immediate hit, with 100+ blue chips signed up and onboarded within 12 months. That is a phenomenal achievement in anyone's book. The new tech was obviously a draw but I'm convinced more than ever now, in a world where we know people essentially buy from people, that the difference was John. He had – has – such passion, such conviction, so much knowledge and to cap it all such all-round good-guy affability that you'd buy from him all day long. Because he cared not just about the sale but making a real success of the project too, helping achieve everything he had promised to the client. It mattered to him. And since we joined forces, he has mattered to us because he's engagement personified. More than that, he actually taught us what this whole engagement thing was about and for that we are very grateful!

## My friend Phil

I've deviated once so I may as well go all in and take the opportunity to introduce the third man, and surely the unsung hero in all of this, Phil Ashworth, Mr Tech.

**MR. TECH**

Phil and I have been mates and colleagues for years. All great double acts have had the yin and yang thing going on, the sort of polarisation that has you wondering how they ever came together until you remember that opposites can so often attract more than they repel.

Phil has two roles in this relationship. One is the indefatigable and hugely talented technical maestro, who in his inimitable unshowy fashion just builds blindingly brilliant software and apps. And who does it in the face of an annoying jack-in-the-box (guess who) who is always asking for more, for different, for next level, blithely unaware of exactly what it takes to develop and deliver showstopping tech. Phil's equanimity serves us well at every turn, not least when prospects are seeking reassurance or fellow techies are demanding answers. He is always the calm, knowledgeable, unflappable figure, who strides like a colossus over the dev and service teams. From day one, he's had this innate feel for what engagement apps should be, drinking in from the well of social media and the competitive market to deliver the optimum combination of looks and functions. He just gets it – which was very handy when I kept popping up asking for more, more, more.

The second role is as my business partner, friend, foil, curber of enthusiasm but loyal and committed backer. He lets me have my head – the enthusiastic puppy on the extension lead – but will not hesitate to rein me in and challenge my thinking But at the end of the day, and when it really matters, you can't put a fag paper between us, because we are absolutely bonded to one another.

**MR. DIGITAL**

Here at Engage and previously at Rekoop, it isn't one Phil at work. These achievements aren't mine alone, they belong to us both. Along the way, you always have doubts, you suffer setbacks, you sometimes question whether you want to carry on. Having a partner who gets you through those times is something very precious. And unlike so many entrepreneurial double acts, it's a relationship that has endured and strengthened – with more chapters to come.

## A moment in time

The business that Intapp bought was Rekoop – memorable not just for its pink branding long before candy colours went mainstream but for being a genuine disruptor in the legal technology arena. When my friend and long-time collaborator cum partner-in-crime Phil Ashworth and I first posited the idea of a Blackberry-based mobile time recording app for lawyers, back in 2009, we were just laughed at. It would never fly, Carpe Diem had the market locked up, there was no way a small start-up would break in and build any sort of user base. But we pressed on regardless and did break through - and very successfully, because we anticipated a need and engineered a solution at just the right...time.

Blackberry took the legal profession by storm and obviously, with so much client work now being conducted on the move, the ability to record that effort instantly via an app (and for lawyers billing by the hour, time captured is money earned!), rather than scribbling it down on your jotter to fill in at your desk later, that ability went down a storm – and our sales went up. We repeated the trick with iPhones and bizarrely ended up with thousands of users who had both iPhones and Blackberrys in play, testimony to the latter's enduring appeal.

At our backs, propelling us forward all the time was that clear digital vision: with the help of the latest technology, we wanted to automate the production of the timesheet. But as time went on, and more law firms started to embrace our approach, I wanted to push further (this will be a recurring motif, you have been warned!). The thing is, we had a unique data set of law firm effort and how profitably – or not - that effort was being utilised. We could legitimately ask the question: you have expensive, skilled resource here – how well is it being used? That opening gambit took me more into the world of Human Capital Management (HCM), with boardroom conversations that frequently touched on engagement inside and outside of a firm. The 'day in the life of a lawyer' became a staple agenda item and helped create and frame some new legal business thinking...and while I didn't know it then, obviously, it was IP that was to prove very useful down the line.

The sale of Rekoop to our main rival Intapp was vindication not just of our business strategy but also our personal decision to back ourselves. Some people, when they are told they can't do a thing, just go and do it anyway but in a sort of petulant spirit, the 'sod it, I'll show them' reaction. That's not really me; I genuinely believed we had an opportunity to do things differently and better and I wanted to test that idea – and my own abilities – in the white heat of a part self-capitalised, part PE-backed business.

The actual specifics – that it was, in the scheme of things, a very niche solution in a sector that I admittedly knew nothing about – those specifics didn't matter half as much as the pure entrepreneurial spirit that made me brave enough - or foolish enough – to nurture this germ of an idea, watered by my innate interest in digital tech. That spirit and belief, and the support and technical brilliance of Phil A, saw us ride the wave all the way from Manchester to Silicon Valley – the original home of computing to the adopted home of computing. In those early days we were not committed to a standard earn-out exit although we had slipped very easily into Intapp's time practice to lead it; the Intapp exec team was welcoming and generous and keen to talk longer-term and both Phil and I loved the injection of a new dynamic: new people, places, thinking and ambitions. In one sense, this was living the dream, the seeds of which had been firmly planted in my early upbringing.

My dad is one of life's polymaths, an engineer by profession and curious and relentlessly inquiring by nature. My childhood coincided with the workplace IT revolution that saw computing power transfer from mainframes and dumb terminals onto the desktop - we were still a long way from the PC World era though, this was strictly the preserve of business. But my dad was fascinated and brought it into the home, tinkering in his study at weekends to build his own PC.

Now a man of a certain age having in his possession a catalogue called Asian Sources might get the odd funny look these days! But back then it was a gateway to untold riches - a panoply of cases, power supplies, motherboards, processors, VGA cards, serial ports, floppy drives, memory, and every other component and peripheral you can imagine. As parts arrived and the project took shape, literally, I was allowed a sneak peek: as my dad explained things, I was instantly bewitched by the potential that sat in the metal box before me, its inherent facility to enable and how that could change everyday things. Like producing my homework. I was the first one in my class to hand in projects put together on a computer (That might explain why I didn't win the Most Popular Kid in School award.)

The nascent nerd became the geeky undergraduate who walked into halls not with the de rigeur hi-fi or Fender guitar, but the custom-built tower PC. And he in turn became the Masters student who did his dissertation on tracking and analysing gym-based performance data - about 10 years before Technogym. If a graduate programme with BT hadn't beckoned (at that time there was probably no richer environment for me to learn how technology could enhance a business), who knows, I could have beaten them to it...given my adulthood love of cycling and addiction to apps like Zwift and Strava, I often wonder what might have been. Maybe that's what's fuelling my passion now though...that sense of making up for an opportunity missed.

Back in Silicon Valley, opportunity still seemed to be knocking. Intapp was a very different style of operation but there was excitement in the pure contrast – and all the learning, the new ideas, the growth plans, the Stanford educated mega brains we were sitting around the table with, Phil and I loved it. Until the point when we didn't.

As time went on, there was just that classic realisation – this simply wasn't us. Us was cycling in the rain in Manchester, us was taking a bit of a mad idea and running with it, us was getting hands on and stuff done, us was being digital tech entrepreneurs and backing ourselves to succeed when others would scoff and say 'you've got no chance'. We wanted another chance. We wanted to be back in charge of our own destinies. We wanted to give something, anything another go because 'autonomy plus challenge' is the thrill that gets you up in the morning. So back we flew to Manchester, leaving San Francisco in 90-degree sunshine, to be greeted by storm force winds and flooding.

We couldn't have been happier.

## Misters and basics

Because of Rekoop and the fact that what started as a mobile app ended up impacting a whole sector, I was perhaps more alive to the potential of the apps John was delivering. Yes, we could certainly enhance the mechanics of engagement within and around a company, that was a given. But was there also the opportunity to transform their thinking, in the way we had with legal, and bring lasting change to more sectors? That would be very cool indeed.

We didn't hang about. The deal was done, the die was cast, we were back in business - and that business was colleague engagement. It may have been a mix of minds and a blend of Misters at the outset, but it was a harmonious collaboration and we were soon focusing on just four things – three research statistics and one observation. These laid the foundation for everything that came after pretty much, so what were the figures that fascinated?

- Companies with engaged employees outperform those without by a whopping 202%
- Some 80% of workers don't sit at desks every day
- 40% of all deskless/non-desked employees "don't feel loved" by their employers

Just three stats but what a world of lost opportunity they painted. Here was a form of digital apartheid, the 'happy haves' with their desks and email/intranet connections to the organisation; and the 'unhappy have-nots', on the frontline, not necessarily equipped with any means to stay plugged in to what was going on, or at least to be able to do so easily and regularly.

**What is colleague engagement and why does it matter?**

In a nutshell, colleague engagement is the connection that colleagues/ employees feel toward their place of work. This is as good a description as I have read anywhere:

> **"Colleague engagement is a workplace approach resulting in the right conditions for all members of an organisation to give of their best each day, committed to their organisation's goals and values, motivated to contribute to organisational success, with an enhanced sense of their own well-being."**

Colleague engagement is not the same as employee experience (EX) although the two are increasingly used interchangeably. Strictly speaking, colleague engagement is what you get as a result of delivering a great experience to your workforce ie experience is the input, engagement is the outcome.

That means there are a huge number of influential touchpoints in play, everything from just the low-level day-to-day organisation/ occupational stuff to the more significant factors like pay and conditions, line manager relationships, integrity of the board, conducive working environment, personal development opportunities etc.

Which all helps to explain why there is no silver bullet for improving colleague engagement – but that doesn't mean we shouldn't try.

## The benefits of colleague engagement

**43%**
**Increased** productivity

**Improved** staff well-being and satisfaction

**Heightened** staff retention and advocacy
**87%** likely to stay in post

**40%**
**Reduction** in absenteeism

**More** personal and professional development

**20%**
**Increase** in sales

**Sharpened** profitability
**21%** increase

**Reduced** costs associated with staff churn

**20%**
**Increase** in customer service and loyalty

**More effective** organisational change

**70%**
**Fewer** accidents in the workplace

**Improved** quality of product/service
**40%** fewer defects

Regardless of which website or report you're on, you'll see a glut of impressive research stats to back all these up. But we come back to the fact that HRs already know what there is to be gained – their challenge, given our earlier note observation about the complexities and subtleties around EX, is far more about how to make it happen for their organisation.

Here was our first take-out. Effective engagement demanded organisational egalitarianism and digital equality. If you didn't equip everyone with the same technology or opportunity, you were doomed before you started. So we had our first base: putting an app on everyone's smartphone (with a complementary app for desktop users too) to end the apartheid, to address the disconnect and get everyone enabled, engaged and empowered.

Added to that was our instinctive take on the situation. The challenge as we saw it wasn't so much pushing the benefits of engagement – all those blue-chips instinctively got why it's a 'good thing' – but how to make a demonstrable success of engagement projects. The early soundings that we took accorded with John's experiences and insights when he talked with prospects – many manifesting understandable 'once bitten' defensiveness: programs were getting launched with fanfare, only to fizzle out; some never even got off the ground at all. Apps were coming and going, all too limited, too disjointed, too orphaned to embed themselves properly or ever to be loved really.

I recall one of the slides we used in sales presentations back then, charting the 'lament' of HR directors faced with making a success of engagement:

**"Where do I start? What do I do next? What are the levers I need to pull? How do I link things together? Why does it have to be so difficult? Why won't my IT team help? How do we drive digital adoption? How do we make sense of all the systems we have? What does success even look like?"**

Wow, the knowing nods and resigned smiles we got when that popped up on screen. But the great thing was that on the next slide we had an answer for them

**The Five Pillars of Engagement**

Look at the Engage website today (www.engagesolutionsgroup.com) and you won't see a reference to the Five Pillars. They were an early construct but while they may have dropped from our marketing toolkit (or rather, morphed into more sophisticated frameworks which we'll come onto later) they are still very much part of our internal vocabulary, and indeed of our coal-face work with clients.

But back in the day the Five Pillars approach was the catalyst – for quicker, clearer understanding; for faster, better, more sustainable roll-outs; for getting us over that first critical hurdle; for putting in the foundations for enduring colleague engagement success.

Our very first job as a new team was to sit down to map out the challenge: what is engagement, its key components, what does success look like, and how do we provide a framework to get there. Or put another way, how do we give clients the clear strategy and enabling mechanism to help them deliver engagement success. In the BP era (Before Phils), John had already done a tremendous job of showcasing his first-generation employee app – it offered so much in such a handy modern package that clients lapped it up: a point solution to a singular problem.

But what came next? Without on-going support or indeed a more fundamental appreciation of how to align the app with business imperatives, then there was always that risk of more failed and aborted projects, with increasing cases of 'twice bitten' HRs. So much of what we saw in those early days gave us pause – whenever we went into a prospect there appeared to be no clear framework within that business that set out out how technology and systems could create engagement success. With real tangible metrics and defensible return on investment figures.

The market at this time (between the encouraging splash of John's first-gen app and the launch of the Engage nextgen app) featured a lot of talk about 'pillars of engagement'. But there was never any agreement on how many there were or should be; there was no consistency in how they were described; and worse, no-one was using them in any meaningful, pragmatic way - for example, as a structure that usefully defines engagement from a disciplines/activities and technology/tools perspective. We made our choices based on a very simple beliefs system: in our world there were five engagement fundamentals and if you focused solely on these you'd be 90% of the way to engagement success.

Our mantra back then was along the lines of not having to boil the ocean. But not being so narrowly focused as to have negligible impact either. Instead concentrate on doing five key things really, really well:

- Communications
- Accessibility
- Enablement
- Recognition
- Feedback

Those five elements were instantly familiar to everyone we talked to. They understood them, they got their value – individually and collectively – and they felt comfortable working in this sort of well-defined, familiar space. That was a massive win right there. And for us back at the ranch, they let us structure our conversations, steer our approach, and shape our technology as we looked to the next-generation version of the colleague app.

From that moment the Five Pillars concept was enshrined in Engage. If we'd been a stick of rock, you'd have found Five Pillars in those little wonky letters running through us. Every business case was based on the 5Ps. Our technology development was defined by the 5Ps. The app was designed with tools that let you do everything 5Ps. What is it about five with us?

We soon had the 5Ps pitch down pat.

> **"Our engagement success teams help you extend and optimise your engagement capabilities - but it's always grounded in the five-pillar philosophy. From the off, pillars give you a guiding hand, a starting point and an onward route. Given the catalogue of failed engagement projects out there, that either didn't know how to start or where to go next or were simply overwhelmed by complexity or expectation, it is something to have a pragmatic route laid out - and the technology to make it happen."**

That was pretty much the gist, and when we ran through it you could see the penny drop – for some HRs it was like having a lifeline thrown to someone drowning, for others it presented the opportunity to be the hero: successfully driving change and improvement where others had fallen short.

There was something else we liked about our pillar selection - and that something was immediate impact. They all offered the chance to change things out of the gate. Too many engagement solutions and strategies offer the promise of positive outcomes - but only after months and months of data gathering and analytical insight, recommendation and sign-off, implementation and evaluation. That's a long time waiting for improvement and payback; why can't impact be immediate, why can't you make a positive difference to both individual and organisation from the get-go? For anyone who has struggled to get traction with engagement and to get the results that they can take to the boardroom, it's good to know that there is another way.

*"I PROMISE, THIS IS THE LAST TIME WE USE PROPS INSTEAD OF POWERPOINT!"*

As I mentioned earlier, the Pillars have since morphed into new style frameworks, ones that honour their origins but now provide that important delineation between internal and external engagement and tell engaging stories to the relevant personas. The Pillars are still in play behind the scenes, still core to our thinking, still providing the solidity and stability, the clarity and cohesion that they have always done.

But critically back then, with that groundwork done and fixed, we could spread our wings a bit as we focused on continuous improvement and enriching our nextgen colleague app. We'd sorted the tools, they were their own eloquent salesman, with twenty features providing a high degree of enablement and efficiency straight out of the box. However, in an app head-to-head there were new entrants who could compete, and potentially knock us out of the running before we were even aware of it. We needed something more, another differentiator, another clever bit of reinvention that could catch the eye, pique the interest, secure us our place on the shortlist.

What we came up with has defined us – and our tech – ever since.

### Pillar talk

Back in 2018, I had an earlier dabble with engagement authorship as I was keen to make the case for the Five Pillars of Engagement – explaining the theory behind the selection as well as highlighting how well they were performing in the real world. I'm not going to reproduce the whole text here but there is a substantial part worth sharing, not just because it's all still relevant today, but also because it evidences how very invested we were from the outset in solving the engagement challenge. There was logic and rigour in our thinking, we saw it as genuine if still evolving IP, not some handy marketing device.

It also gives me a great excuse to dig out a very early creative treatment. We wanted to bring the pillars to life with more than just formal descriptors and diagrams so we commissioned a set of cartoons from UK cartoonist 'Dink'. Well, he just nailed it in true 'pictures paint a thousand words' style and in five frames visually articulated the employee engagement challenges as we saw them back then. HRs loved them and they always made us smile too, hence why we've brought him back to help illustrate the book. Here are ones he made earlier!

**Taken from Engagement Essentials Explained**

We have introduced the Five Pillars of Engagement, a fundamental construct that shapes both our thinking and our technology; but above all serves as a pragmatic framework on which to build engagement success on the ground.

The platform that Engage has developed underpins that framework but now's the time to deconstruct things a bit and talk about singular elements of engagement. Each pillar needs to be relatable; people need to know how they translate into actions and results.

### Communications

Let's take pillar #1 first, communications - the most obvious and most potent weapon when it comes to driving connectedness and cohesion.

Communication is about transmitting and receiving, discussing and understanding: from the broadcasting of company news to the targeted push of information to individuals or teams, to the conversations and collaborations within social networks. But managing effective, timely communications across a large distributed entity is a big ask. Bigger still if half your staff are never going to see that all@ email because they're nondesked or mobile – or just too busy to check.

When we were looking at the tech that would help organisations rise to these various challenges, we simply focused on the basics that would give form and strength to the communications pillar.

We needed to map tools to functions, enabling users to:

- Orchestrate tailored, timely messaging across a large, dispersed organisation quickly and easily
- Use universal or granular push notifications to get the right information in front of the right people at the right time
- Encourage social networking behaviours to help build social capital and strengthen internal communities
- Allow an organisation to connect on a one-to-many, one-to-one, top-to-bottom, bottom-to-top, and all-ways basis

**"GO ROUND AGAIN,
BRISTOL AND MANCHESTER WERE
LOOKING THE WRONG WAY!"**

With tools duly mapped to functions, and a set of comms utilities developed, how did they come off the drawing board and perform at the coal-face? Just how are people using these tools in their everyday working world? How are they standing up the communications pillar?

Let me share a few examples drawn from our customer base to illustrate the 'building' work going on.

There's the retailer whose staff magazine was being produced at obscene cost in terms of both time and money. And yet readership rates were woeful at sub 40% so they effectively app-enabled the magazine through our platform, ensuring key content got to everyone on the frontline directly - and in a timely fashion so the news was still actually news!

A food manufacturer with multiple sites was previously reliant on its site managers and their written blogs for basic engagement with staff. They were available digitally and printed out but were often missed by the non-desked, while those that did read them started to tune out the rather flat, repetitive statements. Now that videos can be easily watched by staff via the Engage app, the site managers are switching to vlogs and thinking more carefully about content, like interviews with staff. By delivering freshened up content in a new medium that people are happy to consume, and that critically gets to everyone equally, the company has given engagement a real shot in the arm.

We're working with a very well-known English football club that on a regular basis has to mobilise, manage and monitor a small army of casual workers. The only way - until now - to ensure they connect with everyone in time has been to deploy SMS messaging; it's very costly, quite unwieldy and pretty limited.

Moving to push notifications as part of a broader platform is changing the game for them: there are no additional costs; curated messages can be put together quickly and go to set groups at the touch of a button; links to key resources can be included so everyone can get what they need from within the app; HR, operations and L&D can all use the same system for their different needs; and there's auditing and analytics so they can better marshal the army and keep behind training, compliance, no-shows etc.

Finally, we have an automotive specialist with multiple sites around the UK. Previously their technicians had worked very much in their own site silo, with a monthly written report coming in from senior head office staff just collating news, service data and product information. It was quite isolating, quite frustrating.

With Engage's social networking capabilities, they've now set up a group-wide technicians' community where they can share, ask, discuss, help, anything that supports the aim of being supportive and constructive; the written log now gets sent out via the app after the new monthly 'town hall' with senior technical staff, where issues can be aired and ideas or upcoming changes can be briefed in.

In just under a year, **technicians' job satisfaction** has leapt by 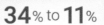 55+% points

and the **leaver attrition rate** has been brought down from 34% to 11%

## Accessibility

As pillars go, accessibility is an interesting one in our book because it is the one that sits furthest away from the traditional employee engagement space of surveys and reward and recognition programmes. But it is also central to our particular view of engagement as we argue for an approach that embraces everything that makes for a happier, more satisfied and more effective workforce and a more connected, efficient and dynamic workplace. Because logic and evidence tell us that engaged, motivated staff boost productivity, workplace stability and cultural contribution more than those who are disengaged.

But also, and just as importantly in our view, because a distributed enterprise that is in tune with its individuals, teams, departments, and sites and is able to build a more joined-up, unified and functional operation, will also see significant performance gains.

This is why we don't talk about employee or colleague engagement as such, it's a bit too narrow - we're see engagement through HR, operational and organisational lenses, with the onus on connectedness, community, culture and cohesion.

And when you look at the issue of accessibility it's amazing how easy it is to inadvertently undermine engagement efforts by just making things much more difficult or awkward than they need to be.

It's always going to be hard to get commitment or best efforts from staff when they feel that they are not getting the same from the organisation. And this is rarely about the big picture, this is invariably all about the small stuff, those day-to-day attritional nuisances that erode morale and frustrate performance, as well as elevating risk, waste and customer dissatisfaction.

Let's be clear, every day staff need information ready to hand - from telephone numbers to duty rosters, health and safety materials to training schedules, company handbooks to corporate directories. Intranets and Sharepoint fall short of being a universal solution if half your workforce - non-desked and without a company email or log-in - can't access them. Ditto any other central system you rely on to keep people informed and in touch.

"A MOBILE SOLUTION FOR COMPANY RESOURCES, THEY SAID..."

I'll cite three examples that I think illustrate their value perfectly. There's the large industrial services firm that's managing 150 engineers across UK client sites.

It once estimated that its field staff were losing anything up to between 30-45 minutes each day through lack of simple, quick access to the occupational resources they needed to do the job.

With that time recovered with our help, **service call productivity has gone up** 15%

We have a manufacturer with five locations, which had experienced a sharp spike in accidents and H&S related incidents following some internal changes and quite wide-scale recruitment.

We came in as part of the remediation plan, both for our comms ability and the fact that we could make resources, guidance and learning tools available to everyone through a single platform.

Finally, we have a major import and logistics operation who was experiencing the classic frustration of multiple systems, effectively siloed, and with nothing to knit them together in a way that could be easily consumed by a very mobile workforce.

They told us that the pressure of having to interact with lots of different systems to get the job done meant that they were getting more resistance and less and less traction from staff; it was a pain, it was morale-affecting, and also gave them significant operational issues as they were getting incomplete data through.

The ability to now link to and 'hub' their key systems, giving users just the single interface for accessing everything they need, has signalled a massive shift in behaviour and mood.

At the end of the first quarter with the new platform in place, the client polled the staff on whether the move had improved things for them to some degree - a lot, moderate or little.

What we are focused on here, remember, are those things we see as the absolute fundamentals for engagement success. If you do nothing else, just do these things well and you will be up and running.

## Enablement

Our third pillar, enablement, sits deliberately in the middle of our five-pillar framework because it is uniquely pivotal and powerful. It also represents the perfect intersection of employee experience and operational effectiveness, which we regard as equally valid parts of the engagement equation.

Admittedly, the introduction of more self-service options is unlikely to drive up the old commitment dividend, and get people revved up about their role and purpose; but it is going to remove lots of little annoyances and inconveniences and time-consuming sidebar activities.

Making enquiries about payslips, tax codes or pensions; filling out forms to update personal details; requesting shift changes; making holiday requests; managing absence; booking training, all of these and more can eat into time and goodwill, especially in a consumer world where 24/7 self-service is increasingly the norm.

The issue with lots of little things is that they can add up to one big thing - loss of productivity, erosion of morale, growing resentment,

"WELL, YOU DID ASK US TO SPEED THINGS UP A BIT."

a negative workday experience that can be very corrosive if left unchecked. That's from the employee perspective; now think about the back-office teams who have to process all this stuff.

Is it really a good use of resource and money to be printing and posting out 1000 payslips? Ditto to send out letters confirming/ updating employee details twice a year? To have someone spending half their week answering basic pay queries? And the other half trying to marshal holiday requests to ensure adequate cover is in place?

We've found all these scenarios in play in recent months and we're now trying to address them because as it stands no-one wins: employees are not getting the frictionless support service that they might expect as standard in this day and age, and organisations are wasting time, money and skilled overhead in the execution of inefficient processes.

What's particularly interesting about enablement is that while it may not be the sexiest of things - let's face it, most of what we're scooping up here is mundane - the business impact is immediate and significant.

**The Engage platform has a ready integration for digital payslips - that has enabled one client to immediately slash £30K from its finance and administration budget**

Employees can now access their payslip history and tax code on demand; and the hours saved on payslip admin every month have been freed up for staff to, amongst other things, monitor a dedicated message/ chat facility. This is allowing for a faster, more responsive approach to specific enquiries, where previously employees could feel like their queries had fallen into a black hole.

Another client has gone a step further, integrating Engage with its own elearning platform to allow employees to dial-up training on demand. It runs quarterly H&S refreshers for all factory floor staff and rather than scheduling sessions that haul people off the floor or impinge on lunch hours, they're delivering it via videos, with employees able to watch them at a time to suit. The system allows for auditing of who has watched what and when, so the training team can direct their focus accordingly

Another client with a big service organisation has also been able to transform its incident alerting procedure. Previously a half manual, half electronic system that saw a timelag of up to a fortnight before advice notifications could be sent out to the rest of the workforce, now a completely automatic, same day solution: Engage allows for instant reporting from the employee involved, which is triaged centrally and an advisory alert pushed out if necessary.

The client involved estimates at least a £25K saving in time alone but puts far more value on the slicker information service it is now providing to protect staff.

**Saving in Time £25k**

### Recognition

Now there was a moment when I thought about tackling this first. Why? Because very often when I sit down with HR heads, the second question I get after 'Can it connect everyone to everything? is 'Can we link to our rewards portal?'

Sometimes it seems like engagement is just a synonym for recognition. Get your employees signed up to some sort of promotional cum loyalty scheme and interacting with it on a regular basis and that's it, engagement job done. But we know proper engagement is far more expansive and complex than that - that's why we developed the framework in the first place. That said, reward and recognition is still fundamental - but it's a part rather than the whole.

Moreover, a one-way, top-down rewarding of staff is a very narrow, limited interpretation. I'm sure recipients of gifts or discounted items enjoy getting them but they might view the process slightly cynically - accepting it as a typical corporate tactic. So they may quite willingly take - but not necessarily give back any more. However, because the scheme is being used and people say they like it - who wouldn't? - then that's okay, you can put a tick against the 'Engagement' box and move on.

That was actually the thinking a client shared with me recently. And while they were happy for our Engage platform to link to their third-party benefits provider, that was a five second conversation. What they really wanted to talk about was how to recast recognition, take it from being a corporate 'ploy' to something of real business value.

Thus began a lengthy chat about democratising recognition and building social capital and cohesion through peer-based acknowledgement and rewards. Just think about it for a second – if you give someone a £30 gift voucher it generally has a limited 1-to-1 impact; whereas if that person is recognised and that recognition amplified through the business so that everyone knows, that person feels much more valued. It's a great way to start and has no P&L impact either. A win-win surely?

I shared the story of another client who had been rather taken aback to learn that the most popular tool in the Engage platform three months on from go-live was the Thank You cards. People were actually

REWARDS & INCENTIVES

dink

"LOOKS LIKE OUR REWARDS SCHEME IS ABOUT TO BECOME MORE ACCESSIBLE."

remarking on how chuffed there were to get the nod, not from their bosses, but their friends. "You want to carry on doing your best for them," was how one recipient put it.

Given that friendships at work are known to be one of the strongest factors for staff retention, you can see why colleague approval arguably has more value than corporate largesse. That's also why we put a fair bit of store by encouraging social behaviours across the workforce.

The 'comments, likes and shares' style of community building that drives consumer apps such as Facebook easily translates into an app for the workplace - creating more opportunities for colleagues to connect and come together (on and offline).

We have another client who recently changed how they did their Long Service Awards, now choosing to make it a headline event via the app.

Each award notice is receiving around 350 likes and 100 comments. Previously announcements barely made a ripple in the water. Harder to put a financial figure on for sure, but that said you just know in your gut it's a good thing. Stand up the recognition pillar in your business, put the tech in place so that everyone can benefit, not just the desked, and you've got the transactional effort/reward side of things covered out of the gate pretty much. But you can also start sowing that community seed - democratising awards, socialising achievement and celebrating each other. Yes, it's hard to put a value on that but I sense that, done well, it could be priceless.

**Feedback**

So here we are at pillar five, feedback. I have been asked whether there is any significance in the order of how we pitch our pillars, and there is. It basically reflects the hierarchy of needs, as told to us by clients.

The universal comms challenge invariably leads the way (remember our natural affinity is with distributed, non-desked organisations), closely followed by giving everyone access to everything they need, and then the ability to do things a bit smarter, faster, more efficiently.

That's not to say we're downplaying the importance of recognition and feedback - benefits, incentives, surveys, mood boards, suggestions and the like - but the reality often is that those two elements are already in play, via an existing point solution, and so there's slightly less urgency. Just as long as we can integrate them or supersede them at an appropriate time, that's fine.

"LOOKS LIKE IT'S
ANNUAL SURVEY TIME AGAIN."

With feedback though, there is another reason why we place it last. As much as it's an engagement pillar, it is also a cornerstone, providing as it does that fundamental check on the efficacy of the other pillars. This is where you find out whether your new corporate comms effort, your new employee support programmes, your new self-service help tools have been a hit - or a miss. It's about getting plugged in and attuned, about listening and acting, and keeping a constant finger on the pulse of the organisation.

Ditching the expensive, ponderous annual survey is undoubtedly a big draw for clients. They do get it, they do understand why a shift to ad hoc pulse surveys, regular polling, monthly town halls etc has to be the future. The internet and social media has given us a 'now' world, an 'on demand' environment and lightning quick news making and mood changing.

For companies looking to control the narrative, well, that genie is out of the bottle really - hard to control what is not visible to you, and those private WhatsApp groups or closed Facebook communities which are dissecting your corporate failings will go on unseen and unchallenged.

The one recourse is to focus on what you can control, which is the experience that gives rise to the narrative. But that in turn needs continuous checks and balances, and genuine opinion seeking and action taking to keep things on course, and to ensure adequate time for remediation if things go off track.

And how difficult is it now to ask people to give an immediate view through their smartphone? That said, the real challenge will always remain that of being willing and able to respond and react to what they say quickly - engagement covers the listening bit, but it's down to executive culture and intent whether the acting bit follows. The prize should surely be enough of an incentive - if you improve the experience, the positive narrative will follow.

As I see it, feedback - the asking and listening process - is both the embodiment of engagement (if we're asking, we're interested, right?) but also the practical means to evaluate everything else you're doing. It's about giving everyone in the company a voice, the ability for peers to thank and recognise each other and for that to be socialised widely. Top down, bottom up, peer to peer, even external – feedback is a powerful engagement mechanism that makes a real difference,

It's about staying alert, being agile, doing more of what's working, changing tack if it's not. As pillars go, it may be last - but most certainly not least.

# CHAPTER 4

As a group, we did a lot of brain work to get things as good as they could be. Phil 'Mr Tech' Ashworth led the way, inspired by the same 'levelling up' IT agenda that nearly 40 years before had inspired my dad to bring business tech into the home – except this time it was the other way, with Phil wanting to bring all the glitz and empowerment of consumer IT into a business tech world that felt off the pace from a user perspective.

I never counted the hours that went into all the development prep but I do remember being in a state of permanent awe at Phil's energy, acuity and sheer doggedness. There were any number of key considerations that had to be addressed and requirements that had to be balanced. It was like a fiendish 3D puzzle but Phil just kept moving the pieces logically until he got the solution.

Let's have a quick recap of those. It's pure coincidence that we ended up with 5Fs. Promise.

Functionality - We had to deliver toolsets that mapped to the pillars. If 'communications' is a key discipline and major part of the engagement programme, what tools do you need to be able to offer users? We had to come up with the options and our starting point was all the great tech out there that people use day in, day out. Facebook-esque personal feeds? WhatsApp style messaging? No problem, we just needed to recreate it, with the addition of a private, secure, compliant environment to wrap around it.

Focus – There was so much temptation to go into ideas overload: the more tools the merrier, right? But stuff too many in, causing the user interface to get bloated and unmanageable, that's not a good look. Ditto a mean, limited toolkit – who's going to warm to something that helps you for about 5% of your day? If we were really committed to putting transformational 'power in the pocket', then we had to get the mix just right – a finely judged balance of the essentials and the cream of the 'nice to haves'.

Familiarity – We looked at the popular consumer and business apps, and in particular the bits of those apps that people used regularly and relied on. We flattered through imitation and served up a UX that looked the part – modern, sexy, bold – and that every user felt instantly at home with, regardless of user demographic or IT literacy level. This was 'everyman' tech, universal and ubiquitous.

Flexibility – You show someone the twenty things an app can do off the bat and there's always someone ready to jump in with 'Yes, but can it [insert any number of custom requests from linking in an existing intranet to integrating a payroll system]. We duly anticipated the need, developing an integration capability from day one to honour an extensibility pledge. Besides, we were all about encouraging self-paced journeys: if clients wanted to kick off and then accelerate and build, we needed to give them a suitably architected platform to enable and facilitate that progression.

Form – We've talked about framing engagement, and how our Five Pillar concept was developed to hang an engagement strategy on. It gave definition. We wanted the platform we developed to reflect that, to have a form and clarity of structure that everyone would 'get'. One of the things about large enterprise solutions is that they are sometimes just too much for people to wrangle into play quickly. We wanted a solution that was logical, easy to understand, fast to roll out. What could be simpler than a core 'fast start' solution that covered all engagement bases, delivered early returns and opened the way to further curation and extension with more systems being brought in behind one single sign-on front door.

As time went on, it became increasingly clear that the world of social media was becoming our muse and fuelling Phil's 'levelling up' IT agenda. It showed us how people were connecting, sharing, collaborating, chatting, learning and doing things for themselves in their private lives; and how easy it was to consume content and to educate and amuse yourself and keep up to date, and contribute and interact in turn. It revealed just how clever Big Tech has been in creating this 'now' world of virtual delights and endless dopamine hits. It may be addictive, but it's also hugely engaging. What wouldn't corporates give to be fostering that level of interactivity, networking, relationships, micro human connections that bond everyone together more tightly in their work collective, their colleague community? And if you could extend that out externally too...

Above all, it highlighted what worked, what really grabbed people. If only all that amazing functionality could be taken out of the inherently unsafe, unmonitored, non-compliant public realm and be placed within the safe perimeter of the corporate firewall. Without losing any of its magic.

There was always a risk that people would misinterpret the 'social media' badge, dismissing the app as some lightweight frippery that would just impinge on working time. Fair enough, social media does have certain connotations; but we had prepared our counter-argument.

It had its roots in this excerpt from a blog written by our non-executive director Rod Bulmer. With twenty years of senior service at the Co-op behind him, Rod spoke his own truth – but it was a truth that was to be universally acknowledged.

**"The internet and social media have given us a 'now' world, an 'on demand' environment and lightning quick news-making and mood changing. For companies looking to control the narrative, well, that genie is out of the bottle really – hard to control what is not visible to you and that private WhatsApp group or closed Facebook community that are dissecting your corporate failings will go on unseen and unchallenged. The one recourse is to focus on what you can control, which is the experience that gives**

**rise to the narrative. Engagement programmes are central to that effort, and given their scope and complexity, you need the right tech and the right thinking to underpin them.**

**If I had my time over with today's technology, I would be asking colleagues much more frequently to give their views on products, mood, service, competition, to encourage far more open communication between peers and between exec teams and managers, managers and colleagues. Think minutes, hours and days not months and years. It is very simple to ask people to give an immediate view through their smartphone. But the real challenge is being able to respond and react to what they say quickly - listen and act; listen and act; listen and act; listen and act. Make for a better experience, and the positive narrative will follow."**

There were two things we took from that post. First, that the tools that were potentially being used against organisations in the outside world – via Big Tech's social media and messaging platforms – could be used for good if you had a way to bring them inside the organisation so that issues were more visible, individuals more easily reached, informed and involved, and the narrative more effectively managed. And second, the tech didn't matter a jot if core behaviours and values and operating standards and pay and conditions and corporate culture – all those things that are the weft and warp of the organisational fabric - if they didn't match up.

We have never sold our apps as panaceas for failing companies, or correctives for toxic environments. But for businesses who wanted to get on that engagement journey, who wanted to improve, who were invested in that 'better experience so the positive narrative will follow' vision, we did have an app – and in that app we had 'Social Media for Business' (SM4B).

We started to use the SM4B tag soon after Rod's blog was published. That simple 'for business' modifier proved immensely powerful. Perhaps it legitimised it, taking it from the realm of consumer plaything to something worthy of board-level consideration. Or maybe it just piqued their interest because it was brand new and, as far as we were aware, a unique take on the engagement and communication challenge. Either way, it gave us the opportunity to explain those original influencing factors – functionality, focus, familiarity, flexibility and form – and to show off the resultant app: at once instantly recognisable and yet something excitingly brand new and full of potential. Take a bow, Mr Tech!

"SOMETHING TELLS ME HE MAY HAVE BEEN
AT THE SOCIAL MEDIA TESTING TOO LONG!"

### Social media moves

The attraction of social media sat safely within a corporate network has only grown over the intervening years. The Big Tech platforms lurch from reputational crisis to reputational crisis, with users increasingly disaffected with the virtual world they find themselves in; and while WhatsApp usage in both the private and public sector still goes on shamelessly, even practiced and publicised by our own government, there is, thankfully, a belated awakening to its security flaws and inherent subversion of data protection laws.

At Engage, we've had to play close attention to new trends and platforms: TikTok was launched in 2017 worldwide although it's only in the last couple of years that it has become this gargantuan viral force. And while we don't build mini TikToks or Instagram platforms into the app, we do take note of what these signal from a content consumption perspective; that's why we ensure we always have optimal native support for video and photos and AR filters, and have, more importantly, created the means for these to be uploaded and shared virally by individual users, just as they are on public platforms. Which brings us neatly to social posting.

Until 2020, SM4B consisted of tools that mirrored the social media stalwarts, the most stand-out being the Facebook-style feed and WhatsApp-esque group messaging channels. They allowed a limited degree of those classic social behaviours – commenting, sharing and liking – by employees when reacting to content put out by their employer. Being instant and easy, the set-up encouraged news and information to be spread faster and further; more two-way dialogue and interactivity between the centre and the edge; and it allowed both a quicker reading and more detailed analysis of sentiment and mood. But its enduring value was in being that reliable 'go-to' place to keep your finger on the pulse, and basically to receive rather than give.

In 2020, we launched an updated version of SM4B, with a new feature – what we refer to as 'social posting'. For the first time, we were wholly emulating consumer platforms as everyone in the business could (if permissioned) now post in their own right and build their own followings. We'd had conversations with a few clients who were keen for their internal comms to break free of the convention of just 'broadcasting' via the feed. Even though the feed allowed that social interactivity of sharing, liking and commenting, it still fell short of everyone being able to contribute, and developing their own voice; something that some organisations felt was essential for deeper engagement and for building stronger – and different – connections.

It was one of those fortuitous moments really as that thinking chimed perfectly with ours – it seemed such an obvious extension of the app's capabilities, bringing 'social media for business' ever closer to its consumer twin and encouraging this ultimate version of personal engagement and expression.

I'll confess, I was very excited. I get mesmerised by the shiny and the new and I have every model of iPhone to show for it. The social posting capability was shiny and new – but it also had this incredible potential to take engagement to a whole new level. And as I said earlier in the book, technology's ability to change the game, unlock new worlds and help us envision the 'art of the possible', this was my passion. And I got very passionate about it, and I wanted to take it into every boardroom, the proselytiser-in-chief for SM4B Mark 2.

To give you a better sense of how I felt about it, that this ran far deeper than just having another feature to sell, I'm going to share the transcript of a podcast I put together a few months after launch. The clients who'd independently come to the same conclusions we had, they lapped it up; others were not so sure. I don't know whether I was more frustrated with them for not seeing what I thought was obvious, or with myself and my team for somehow failing to fully articulate the proposition. A podcast seemed a good way to deliver the message with feeling!

**Podcast transcript**

*"Social posting – what do I mean by that? The easiest way to think about it is having within your business the same social networking experience and capabilities as you do in your personal consumer lives – not using public social platforms and apps but your own private, secure, compliant version of these, sitting on the smartphones of every colleague or customer.*

*And why does it matter? Think about it. Social media, it's how we connect with our friends, family, the groups we're part of. TikTok, WhatsApp, Facebook, Snapchat, Instagram, they're all part of our everyday vocabulary, they're driving ever higher levels of engagement. And, of course, they're all-powerful mobile apps - we are now a mobile-first nation with around 70% of internet traffic going through the phone - and, pretty much ALL of the social media interaction and engagement is now via the phone too.*

*So this whole idea of fostering social networks for business has been a major driving force for us here at Engage – we wanted to create the same social network experience so that you could have the same level of engagement with your colleagues, within the safety of your company. To give every member of the company a voice, to create and share exciting and interesting content, to have new conversations and offer ideas and opinions - just like you do with friends and family.*

*Think about that in terms of all those micro connections at a human level that transcend company hierarchies, that break down some of the barriers that inevitably occur because of position and seniority or even just physical dislocation. They help build stronger relationships that are not just predicated on work – people naturally connecting with each other, interacting, sharing, supporting, laughing, that's absolute gold for the collective good, the community spirit, everyone feeling like they're in it together. That positivity, that sense of being invested in* one another, that's a hugely powerful force – it's social capital that can drive performance and growth.

The thing is, technically, most companies don't have the ability to do this – which is exactly why we baked into our colleague engagement app the option for you to create your very own, fully branded social media platform for your business.

And let's talk for a second about other practical gains. This giving people a voice...again, it's immeasurably valuable for feedback and improvement and for gauging the temperature of the workforce. Traditionally, employee apps have been focused on broadcasting – the centre to the edge, the one to many. But you only have to look at the likes of Facebook and WhatsApp to know how much richer, more textured, more interesting communications become when we can all talk freely, and just how much relationships can blossom and strengthen when we have the means to talk, chat, swap videos anytime, anyplace.

Now, what's that I can hear? Ah, it's the trumpeting of the elephant in the room! It's blaring on about the risks of giving everyone the ability to say what they like – as in, let staff loose on social media, are you mad? Trust me, I hear it. I'm having this conversation a lot right now and it's exactly what's inspired this podcast. I've been pushing and pushing and pushing social posting to our own client base based on my own convictions. But there's hesitancy there. And I do understand why, given some of the less edifying aspects to social media that crop up almost daily in the news outlets.

But the fact is, your staff are probably already having these conversations, or chirping their grievances, or just cultivating friendships – but it's happening outside of your view, your control, on public platforms and apps. It's happening in that WhatsApp group, or Facebook page, or community forum. And that's actually the bigger *elephant in the room...it's such a lost opportunity not to be fostering that social connectivity inside your organisation where you can harness it for the good of everyone and the wider business.*

*I recently had the privilege of sitting down with Richard Clark, the CEO of one of our clients, CFG Law. Now if any organisation was going to be alert to or averse to the risks of social media, you'd think it would be a law firm. But Richard has championed social posting from day one and the firm is my default reference for how it can successfully augment and amplify the 'standard' engagement and communication activities. I asked him about the elephant and he didn't hesitate.*

*"If you trust someone enough to employ them, then you should trust them to do the right thing for your organisation"*

*Yes, trusting people to exercise their power or their freedoms responsibly. If you can't do that, then you have far more fundamental problems to worry about than unlocking a new feature on the app."*

## Onside inside

Whatever else you say about social media, it's effortless ability to bring people together and build personal, human connections and collective, community spirit is unquestioned. Its dynamic, interactive and viral quality is pretty much the essence of engagement – you're on the hook, you're interested, you're reacting, sharing, contributing. We do it all day long in our private lives, leveraging the tech available to us. And yet in our business lives, there's no real equivalent. Email is still the default all-hands communication channel, while the likes of Slack, Yammer and Teams are just streams of operational consciousness. Cultural improvers and weavers of the social fabric they are not. And that's exactly why our colleague engagement app was predicated on 'social media for business' in the first place. Those social style tools, instantly familiar to everyone, uber simple to use, powering things like the company feed and secure messaging.

And now we also have social posting in the mix, the opening up of the app so that everyone can be involved, the edge moving freely in and around the centre. It's no longer just about flowing formal comms through the feed, it's about fostering your own social network for your business: bringing people closer, learning more about the colleagues around you, cutting through the layers, reaching across silos, almost like building lots and lots of little connectors between individuals that might not otherwise exist, with a variety of results: a greater collective spirit, a commitment dividend, happier employees because they have found other things, other people in work that they can relate to; a breaking down of 'them and us', reconsidering your opinions of people you have only seen in their glass office but who have now revealed things in their head and their heart. It's not only more social but more humanising too.

There's something else, another fairly weighty dimension to social posting that we all need to be across: it taps into employee advocacy, that externalising of the positive internalised view. Giving your colleagues a voice and freer rein to contribute takes them from passive to active players, from human resources to brand ambassadors. That's an army of fans plugged into all their own personal social networks, unlocking exponential growth in terms of reach and impact well beyond your organisational boundaries.

Research data has content shared by employees to their personal followers on Facebook, Instagram, Twitter, TikTok etc, getting eight times more engagement than when it is posted via a brand's own accounts. It's also shared 25 times more frequently. Seems like having your people onside inside delivers big on the outside too.

# THE CROSSOVER

**CHAPTER 5**

Speaking at a business conference recently I described colleague engagement as the bedrock of a broader engagement program: more than just a 'beginning' to a journey, rather, the absolute foundation stone. But as we took our first steps in 2018, I was still some way off having that clarity of vision. But the more settled the development team became on the nextgen version of what was now to be styled permanently as our colleague engagement app, the more liberated I felt to do a bit more 'exploring'- and, as hinted at in Chapter 1, to extend this new engagement adventure.

One of the things I am most grateful for in business is the people around me. There's a core team here, some of whom I have worked alongside for over a decade in three different organisations. They're all fantastic at their job but they also have something even more valuable – an understanding of me, and how I think and work.

In my spare time, I'm a keen cyclist and if I was drawing on cycling as an analogy for my operating style, I would be that annoying rider who continually sprints to the front of the peloton, breaking away from the pack with a new wind behind me; to be typically followed by a falling back to the pack to try and convince people to come with me. Why weren't they up on my wheel, pedalling as excitedly as I was?

I am sufficiently self-aware to know (it might be all the sighing or eye-rolling that did it) that it can be a frustrating process to be taken from your current task and to be asked to refocus on something quite 'out there'. But the team know how I roll and will be the first to stand up and say that without that continual pushing, that purposeful drive to the front, we wouldn't have got to where we are today.

Yes, maybe some of my idea 'sprints' deserved the eye-roll...but there have been others that have come along and hit the mark. And then we all get on our bikes together to make that happen. I call it entrepreneurial spirit, others might have a less polite term for it! But it's those breakthrough successes that keep you coming back for more.

**"ALL I SAID WAS THAT I'D HAD ANOTHER IDEA!"**

Forgive the little psychology vignette there but it's important for understanding what happened next. We were on our way to developing the best possible colleague app...why not look beyond the internal audience to the external?

I'd already had a little private shake-out of the customer app idea, found nothing untoward dropped out and so it was still very much live. This was late 2018 and I remember having a meeting with a prospect, our first face-to-face with them where we were doing the whole 'getting to know you, how can we help you' bit. Sat across the table from me were the CEO, the operations director, the head of production, and the HR director; we'd already had a positive meeting with the latter, so we had a good read on the situation coming into this session. In a nutshell, we had a manufacturer of specialist vehicles who had found themselves an analogue business in a digital world – and colleague engagement was one part of an anticipated broader modernisation vision and transformation programme.

The fact that we had key members of the C suite sat with us was ample confirmation that this was a solid opportunity and after 90 minutes of a proper interrogative discussion it was clear that we were finding our mark. I had run through the pillar theory and done a quick show and tell of the app; you know that it's all hitting home when a company starts relating it directly back to their own business, throwing out examples of how, say, our messaging tools could improve their inconsistent, cascade-oriented approach to internal comms; or our self-service forms could slash lots of admin time when it came to rota changes and holiday requests. So far, so normal.

I was about to move things on to discuss the merits of our formal discovery process and business case building when the CEO leant forward in his chair and asked: "Can we use this for our customers?"

Now this was an interesting turn of events. Slightly unexpected too, to be honest, as it hadn't come up when we'd qualified the lead originally or in our briefings with HR. But I didn't hesitate.

"Absolutely."

I felt excited and nervous at the same time. Here was someone who'd got to the same place I had and was giving me an open door. It was hugely significant, we had a sniff at reinventing ourselves and becoming much, much more integral to the change process and business growth – and a much larger, more successful organisation ourselves.

I had a clear take on where we were at that point, and how far we'd come. We had started life as the employee engagement app people – ESG had been the first to market and the nextgen app we were now delivering would look to keep us at the front of the pack. From our coal-face experience across a wide range of sectors, we were growing familiar with the trends: companies were struggling with developing a pragmatic strategy when it came to internal engagement. Apps like ours could help - but from what we could see improvements were too often ad hoc and spasmodic and not necessarily aligned with business objectives. What was needed was a coherent phased programme that delivered real, sustained change on the ground, at a pace to suit the organisation, and in a journey that reflected their priorities.

We sat with many HRDs who had great vision and ambition but who also felt overwhelmed by the scale of the task – where did they start, and once started where did they go next? We agreed and we sympathised, and then we went into bat for them – by creating a strategic framework and a technology platform that gave them the map and the vehicle to make a success of their engagement journey.

The starting point had to be the framework. We'd agreed at the outset that not a line of new code would be written before we'd defined something logical, straightforward, coherent, that people would 'get' and be enthused, not overwhelmed, by. Something that would make colleague engagement more manageable, effectively offering up some guiding parameters and limiting the scope. Too often we'd seen people paralysed by the enormity and complexity of the task they saw before them; if we could instead offer up some engagement fundamentals and get minds concentrated on those and those alone, then we reckoned that the engagement elephant – rather than be swallowed whole – could be eaten one bite at a time.

It wasn't rocket science. We were only advocating the old 'doing the basics well' approach when you think about it and that was what had inspired the Five Pillars of Engagement. They would provide a strong backbone and clear direction to an engagement effort: they could be focused on in turn, or all at the same time, or indeed in any number of priority combinations to best suit the needs of the organisation. The most important thing was that it was a framework whose pillars resonated, and accurately reflected the disciplines most likely to shift the needle on engagement.

It was only then that we ramped up the build of the supporting technology. At the front-end we had the user app – powerful simplicity – but at the back-end we had the simply powerful: a platform that not only fed the app but also created the means to integrate other line of business systems and present them on the app.

And it also had another crucial advantage, one that I suspect had caused my mind to wander in the first place: the digital connection and enablement we offered, coupled with a clear strategic framework, why limit that to just an internal audience? Yes, our world up to that point may have been viewed through the prism of HR and internal communications, but was that the only view we were ever going to take?

## Coming round to engagement in the round
It didn't take long to get to a position where we could argue for engagement to be seen rather more holistically – why couldn't everything we were advocating for the workforce be applied equally to customers? Surely we wanted to be able to communicate more effectively and efficiently? To help them have a better experience? To hear their opinions? To acknowledge and reward key clients? To

let them do more for themselves? As I saw it, the framework and platform we had developed could facilitate an effortless pivot from internal to external engagement.

And here I was that wintry day in 2018, sat across the table from a CEO who had independently reached the same conclusion – or hoped he had.

"Absolutely" I replied, with a confirmatory nod and the twitch of a smile. I took my still somewhat inchoate thoughts and tried to order them into a rational, compelling pitch. I probably went on a bit but I got across the main idea, this ability to swing from inward to outward and how you could use the same pillar-based approach and technology - just with intelligent tweaks to tools and content so it was properly tailored to a customer audience.

The CEO looked down at his pad. He'd been scribbling for a while before his question but I'd assumed it was general note-taking. It wasn't. It was a list. The platform we had...could it:

- Alert customers to new stock?
- Send out a company bulletin?
- Publish a product launch video?
- Advise of vehicle delivery dates?
- Let customers access documentation?
- Allow customers to book services and MOTs?
- Have secure messaging for key accounts?
- Offer a service centre directory?

There were others but you get the gist. In fact, subsequent to this meeting, the CEO convened an 'all ideas on the table' session with his full leadership team devoted to seeing how much mileage they could extract from the platform in its customer engagement dimension. By the time everyone had chipped in, they'd generated a list of 40 discrete tasks/functions, across all five pillars/functional areas.

I remember leaving that meeting absolutely buzzing. My roving thoughts had collided with a CEO's live needs, there was a massive win right there. But there was also something else.

When the CEO had loosed off his fusillade of 'could it dos', I'm sure I detected a subtle change of mood in the room. Previously, the meeting tone had been workmanlike, a recognition that they needed to improve things on the colleague front. There were operational necessities too, and our discussions had reflected that. They had tried a few things before, not always successfully, and were now trying again, albeit as part of a more expansive programme for the company. But when we flipped to the customer conversations, it was like a pressure change, a different energy...was there a genuine frisson of excitement?

We had about an hour's more discussion and all parties showed a tangible enthusiasm for what might be possible. As we dug and explored more, it was like peeling back the layers of an onion. The CEO revealed that a couple of his major fleet customers had fed back informally a few months previously that they would welcome some innovation in their customer experience, particularly around communications on stock availability, self-service bookings for MOTs and servicing, and build/delivery schedule updates. Others round the table then offered up a few more anecdotal bits and some thoughts they'd had on the back of them. Good ideas all of them but when prompted as to why nothing had happened, it was more or less the same answer that had brought us to their door in the first place – there was no overarching plan, and no technical capability. Bespoke custom development wasn't something they had any appetite for and tailoring enterprise systems, ditto – hugely expensive, long-winded, risky, horribly draining on time and energy, no, simply not an option.

But a platform with tools that could be used out of the box? That could link other systems together? That could automate and enable? That inherently – through the pillar framework - provided some guidelines as to what was in and out of scope, shaping a plan of action? A platform supported by people who could even do agile development where needed? The same platform they were set to use to help their internal cohort? That potential really got them thinking, and I don't think I was imagining that buzz in the room. When they shared their 40 ideas with us a bit later, I knew for certain.

I appreciate that we have to deal in the nuances of colleague and customer engagement from a practical perspective – it is never going to be one campaign for all obviously. But the fact that the strategic framing and the technological enablement are the same across the board, that is incredibly powerful, enticing and compelling.

After that session I did some further mental kneading of the idea, bringing all of these thoughts together, and knocking them into a clearly defined narrative for the pivot piece. In my head it came down to this:

You have your engagement essentials toolkit that can be used in-house out of the box; can be embedded in any presentation layer eg mobile device, desktop; can be extended seamlessly through integrating other systems; and can even be custom tweaked to drive more differentiation and innovation.

At the right time, you pivot from internal to external.

Same theory, same platform, different audiences, same result – a better experience, a stronger connection, an enhanced capability, more consistent engagement, a bottom-line impact. For the CEO, that's an attractive proposition – getting a return on investment on two fronts and threading a tight skein of mutuality from the workforce up through the C suite and out to the customer.

End-to-end engagement. Could this fly?

Absolutely.

ALL ABOARD

## CHAPTER 6

So this was it. We'd crossed
over to the other side: customer
engagement was now officially
a 'thing'. The client was excited, I
was super excited, and Phil? Well,
he didn't rush to thank me for
obligating him to unlock some busy
development resource to get the
app as envisioned in my head onto
my iPhone – the first iteration of the
Engage customer app.

While there was theoretically a lot of overlap with the colleague app in terms of tooling, we still in reality had to devise a new UX, develop some extra features, explore additional integrations...my natural 'Tigger-ish' enthusiasm that wanted everything next week didn't exactly go down well. But then again, Phil has spent many years putting up with my idiosyncratic wiring and I can rely on him for a cool assessment of any sparking idea. He was quickly on board, as was John – we had first mover advantage again, and Mr Digital, Mr Tech and Mr Engagement needed to press on. Rather ironic then that all this time later still no-one has come close to emulating what we've done. We needn't have rushed...

Trouble was, I was born to rush, to race ahead; it felt like I had a new toy to play with. While Phil and his team locked themselves in a darkened room to produce our first ever customer app for our vehicle manufacturer, I was out and about, talking to anyone who would listen about customer engagement. I needed sounding boards, different voices, multiple perspectives, to be questioned and challenged; the idea needed both further exploration and ultimate validation.

Initially I set up conversations with both food service brands and high street retailers, as that was where we had internal traction and a good market understanding - and it was like someone pricking my balloon. With a really vicious stab of a really big pin. With the growth of omni-channel marketing strategies and increasing spend on digital marketing, I was expecting a totally unprompted enthusiasm for customer apps and the mobile-first strategy that came with them. I thought they would be opening up their cheque book right there. But the more I lobbied for, the harder they argued against. Had I got this badly wrong?

I needed answers so I started digging – I hadn't exactly bet the farm on customer engagement being a winner but there would be some very sleep-deprived developers to deal with if we hit the 'stop'. button. Yes, we had one client enthusing no end, but what do they say about one swallow not making a summer? I needed to find more swallows and fast.

It seemed to me that the 'pushback' brigade split fairly evenly into two camps – let's call them the 'once bittens' and the 'already sorteds'.

The 'once bittens' were fairly straightforward. They were all early adopters of digital and had invested significantly in first generation customer apps. And all their stories were depressingly similar - launched in a flurry of promotional excitement, plentiful incentives to download the app and get on board, a piece of hero marketing content (augmented reality was very flavour of the month, more on that later), the first flush of take-up and interaction, and then a slow withering on the vine, with users disengaging and eventually removing the app.

I totally got it and I even coined a term for it: 'app and throw' - a bit of eye-candy and a big marketing push that gets people's attention for five minutes, but without any sustainable value or merit. If you couldn't keep people engaged for the duration, then you could hardly be surprised that your app was being deleted as quickly as it was downloaded. But the 'once bittens' – having invested so much for so little return - were understandably a tad shy of entering the app space again.

The 'already sorteds' were a little more complicated. They thought they had customer apps covered off, there wasn't anything that I could tell them. Except I could and did, explaining how their loyalty app or ordering app or storefront brand app fell short of my definition of engagement. These apps all shared the same characteristics: they're largely transactional, most of the content is static, they're inactive and inert between transactions and there's no lifecycle management.

In my eyes, what they had was a functional marketing tool – not a relationship-building, value-enhancing engagement mechanism. And without that lifetime investment in the customer, there's always the danger of them losing interest, or being lured away by a competitor or the next new shiny thing. This is what we might term the 'app and go' effect – where the app stays dormant on the phone but the customer has long gone.

My follow-up was to paint a picture of avoidable customer disengagement and a world of opportunity. I talked about our work developing nextgen customer apps – and how we wanted it to be about 'app and grow'. We had to move apps away from the world of throwaway marketing campaigns and one-dimensional transactional stuff - they needed to sit at the heart of the customer relationship.

In our world, customer apps would give organisations the opportunity to own the customer lifecycle end-to-end; to connect them directly to their customers, communicating and supporting them at all times; to anticipate needs - and drive revenues - by improving cross-sell, upsell and resell; to reward loyalty and referrals; and to enhance the whole customer experience through smarter service, innovation and personalisation. And as a clincher, through the very existence of a branded customer space, it would give them another channel to capture prospects right at the top of the funnel, inviting them in and nurturing the conversion.

The onus must be on maximising customer lifetime value - and for that you have to give them a reason to stay for life, not just let them drop out of your world after a single purchase. You need to make people feel special even when they're not spending with you. That's the challenge that nextgen apps are helping with today and that was the case I was making back them. Here was a vehicle for that sustained communication, interaction and convenience, and the chance to be part of a vibrant, exciting brand tribe – not just the means to transact and cash in on your reward points. 'App and grow' was exactly that – strengthening bonds, increasing brand equity, loyalty and advocacy, and growing revenues from both existing customers and those coming in via referral.

I must confess right now that I became an unashamed zealot for this latest piece of disruptive thinking. It filled my blogs and conference slots, and I was endlessly asking our client success team to link me up with chief marketing officers so I could try out my theories. If you were one of those who suffered 'customer engagement evangelist Phil', then my apologies – but I had to know!

"WHEN I SAID A MOBILE-FIRST APPROACH
TO CUSTOMER ENGAGEMENT..."

### Engagement, marketing and CRM

I started off with one central tenet, the crystallisation of all the thoughts and findings I've described above: it was my belief that customer apps were about to enjoy an evolution that would transform them from first generation marketing apps, focused narrowly either on one-shot hero content or transactional mechanisms; to nextgen engagement apps that would enable an organisation to own the entire customer lifecycle, managing the end-to-end customer journey.

Engagement shouldn't be seen as interchangeable or synonymous with marketing. For all the investment made in Customer Relationship Management (CRM) systems, there is little genuine regard for the 'relationship'. Marketing obviously must support the sales cycle, that's the whole point, but a relationship between supplier and customer shouldn't be defined wholly by its purchasing points. The sales offer that leads to the transaction that leads to the 'how did we do' follow up, that's a classic sequence. But then? Nothing. Well, not quite nothing as every couple of months that CRM system will spit out an email. It may or may not be relevant. But here's the thing: there is a very good chance that you will never even know if it was relevant or not.

The current run rates on email marketing – and this is at the higher end of expectations – are open rates of 25% and click through rates of 5%. In other words, some 75% of the intended audience sees nothing and 95% do nothing! And yes, marketeers will tell you that this sort of stuff is all a numbers game but I just don't accept that – it's a waste. It's busy fool syndrome (even busier fools in the Covid era as we experienced the most virulent email plague). It's no-one being prepared to challenge norms and argue for another way, a better way.

Marketing is always about the next transaction – how would you feel if you were only ever contacted by someone who wanted something from you? Who drifted in and out of your life and only got excited to see you when there was a sniff of something in it for them? It's not edifying behaviour in normal life, it's not how friendships, relationships, loyalty and commitment work. Customer engagement is what CRM should have been: that obsession with the end-to-end customer lifecycle that starts at the top of the sales funnel – even before they become a customer – and keeps them in play and live, so that they don't just drop out of the bottom of the funnel to never buy again. And this isn't some touchy-feely woo, this is grounded in hard commercial facts.

A quick illustrative sidebar. A couple of years ago we studied some of the research that was coming out of the legal sector. I've always kept an interest in the space, and I did see it as a potential sweetspot for

Engage. And we came across a remarkable statistic: on average less than 15% of law firm clients go on to take a second service from that law firm. And less than 5% ever make it to that third transaction, or 'matter' in legal parlance.

Wow. All that money spent to attract, and all that money wasted in a devastating attrition rate. In fact, it was worse than that. Just boosting those rates has a clearly calculable benefit in more business won but the revenue impact is even greater. Back in 2016, Harvard Law School's Heidi Gardner produced research that showed when a law firm expands client services to two practices, revenues from that client triple. When we modelled how customer engagement could – at a conservative estimate - double the 'one to two' rate, we were able to evidence a £2.5m revenue gain for a £20m SME law firm. At its heart, all we were doing was system-enabling the ability for the firm to keep in touch, to anticipate client needs by offering them relevant additional services, and to encourage actions and attitudes generally that would make clients feel valued at all times – not just when they had cause to solicit more advice.

But back to revolutionising the customer relationship and redefining marketing – just a couple of small tasks to be polished off before lunch! Seriously though, the potential of this nextgen, customer engagement-inspired approach to reframe how we connect with and relate to our customers is huge. Up to now, an organisation has deployed an omni-channel strategy to first attract and convert, and to then keep in touch with their customer: email, direct mail, SMS, phone, website, social media and, in some instances, a first-generation app (as noted previously, typically limited to loyalty mechanisms or one-shot promotional concepts). That's a lot of effort to stay connected to someone who is already invested in you as a customer. And we've already seen that 95% of email effort goes completely unrewarded.

Swapping out that first-gen marketing app or moving directly to a true customer engagement app lets you change things up significantly: a bit less omni, a lot more optimal. Nor do you have to write off your CRM investment − it is simply repositioned as the data workhorse backend, fully integrated and feeding the sexy, dynamic front end.

With the recalibration of mindset and mechanics done, you now have an app that ceases to be one channel of many, operating on the periphery; instead it moves into the centre to take control of the customer relationship.

It is your direct, 'no filter' route to your customer, keeping them closely connected, supported, and informed at all times. Your brand presence is right there on the home screen, your relationship constant and enduring − if properly invested in and nurtured, of course. All relationships need working at! I've always argued that it's the next best thing to having them in the room with you. Which means that so much else of what you do - the email rounds, the direct mailers, the texts, the calls - becomes, if not exactly superfluous, then certainly not so necessary. You have a live one-to-one connection via the app - you can't improve on that.

Having customers interacting within a single homogenous environment also has the advantage of opening up a new data analytics front. Tracking behaviours and interactions and crunching a mass of data points can facilitate the sort of micro personalisations that customers love − and which brands can serve up effortlessly through the app. It's a virtuous circle of relationship management, with the potential to endure for years, not just weeks and months.

And in a way it perfectly encapsulates the change every organisation needs to make: stop focusing purely on the sales cycle - the here and now; and start obsessing about the customer lifecycle - the here and forever.

## Catalytic conversers

The good news is that the 'pushback' brigade of both stripes has itself been pushed back. Receptivity is replacing resistance, there are increasingly more enthusiastic brush strokes around the 'art of the possible' as C teams get comfortable with the concepts. Best of all, we've already been party to new customer eco-systems being developed on the strength of our customer engagement app. Detailing each one would take another book but I just want to highlight some of the aims and ambitions that kick-started various client conversations so you can better understand the initial impetus for deploying the app.

Five quick examples for you:

A specialist insurance company wanting to create a complete end-to-end experience for policyholders, from self-service renewals and claims tracking to purchasing of policy add-ons to a community-style wrap of special interest groups (motorbikes, classic cars etc), events and promotions.

A law firm looking not only to give clients 24/7 access to case progress with messaging options but to automate the cross-selling process by introducing other key contacts (eg family team to someone taking conveyancing services, employment team to a business owner taking M&A advice) at appropriate milestones; and to enable new clients to get quotes and self-incept matters.

A custom vehicle manufacturer needing to make a significant analogue to digital transition so it could retain customers with a raft of convenience measures: booking services, alerts on MOTs falling due, checking in on build status, weekly stock updates, new vehicle videos with augmented reality sequences.

An automotive parts supplier wanting to augment its largely telephone-based sales/ordering operation by creating a useful, enjoyable in-app experience for its garage customers, featuring the Parts Guru, delivery alerts, stock updates, promotional offers, marque-oriented messaging channels, Apprentice of the Year competition and a fantasy car photo gallery.

A leisure chain keen to move its existing customer-oriented tools from its website to a mobile app and to add in more features to drive both retention and acquisition – class calendars and booking, 'refer a friend' codes, performance leagues, personal trainer videos, digital membership cards, self-service membership renewal, self-service guest passes, suggestion box, member of the month competition, charity chooser poll.

## New frameworks explained

Our customer engagement app emerged fully formed in mid-2019. Its arrival put the next step of the engagement journey on the map. It now had this new pivot point, switching from internal to external audiences, but in essence replicating all the same engaging behaviours and offering the same degree of enabling technology to B2B and/or B2C customers.

At that time we were still rolling with the Five Pillars. They had served us really well, providing that strong, coherent framework that helped everyone understand the pieces of the engagement puzzle more readily. But with two apps came two audiences and multiple different personas to influence. We needed to freshen up our own presentation to delineate things more clearly. Given the marketing orientation of our new audience, we also had to stretch our creative legs. We wanted an approach that would land, resonate, and cut through the noise, something bold and simple enough to grab hold of, but not simplistic. It had to cleverly capture just how transformative we could be, and just how transformed our clients could be. What we developed respected the Five Pillars credo – we just reimagined it for the extended engagement journey.

Colleague engagement is today articulated through the REACH framework; customer via the COURSE framework. And we love showcasing these, not in a show-offy way but because people get them quickly and they're straight off into their own worlds, seeing their organisations through this lens. That makes for lively, honest, insightful chats when we're together, and even better, you can see the opportunities emerge, and the excitement build.

Time to share!

# Powering colleague engagement

## REACH out and connect your firm

- **Re-engage** with all colleagues desked and non-desked, and encourage and empower them to play their part in the company's success

- **Provide easy access** to all the occupational resources and support your colleagues need to do their job efficiently, safely and compliantly

- **Automate** tasks to encourage smarter working, self-service and self-help enhancing experience and convenience at the front-end, improving efficiency at the back

- **Continuously** improve the business through real time feedback, suggestions, two-way dialogue and robust measurement of progress- give your colleagues a voice and visibility of the mission and their role

- Invest in a **healthy,** energised workforce, and champion wellness, equality, learning and development- reward effort, celebrate achievement, help and acknowledge your peers

# Powering customer engagement

## Set your customer journey on the right COURSE

- **Convert** more new customers by surfacing the app on social and web, bringing them into your branded community as clients-to-be

- **Own** the customer lifecycle, not just the transaction, and obsess about relationships and lifetime value

- Drive **upsell,** cross-sell and resell by automating future sales opportunities to encourage customers to buy more and/or buy again

- Get the most out of customer **recommendation** and satisfaction, system enabling referrals and loyalty rewards to boost both retention and acquisition

- Empower customers with fast, convenient **self-service** and self-help options, letting them order, book, check, research and update details 24/7

- Always deliver a great customer **experience,** creating more wow through innovation, personalisation and stand-out content

CHAPTER 7

With the official launch of the
Engage customer app we became
a binary play. It was very simple:
we did colleague apps and we did
customer apps. Naturally symbiotic,
yes, but as deployed in real life,
typically discrete programs with
separate sponsors and success
criteria. The engagement vision that
we'd had in early 2018 was now
complete in late 2019.

Which gave me a problem. The design and development, the workshopping and testing, the pricing and the pitching, they'd been all consuming for months, for me and for the whole team. Customer was the main course to the colleague app's entrée and together they represented two years of maximum effort and hard yards. The launch only ramped things up for the team but I was finally able to step back, dial down the intensity for a bit. And suddenly I had a vacuum... we'd designed and delivered two nextgen apps, we were two years older and wiser...but now what? Forget nature abhorring a vacuum, my nature abhors one too, to about the power of ten. Remember my cycling analogy from earlier? This was me sat in the peloton, brooding about when and how to make my next break forward. But then, as I debated with myself about how to fill the imminent void – and others worried about how I would! - we started having some slightly different conversations with people.

These were largely stimulated by the new customer app push. I remember they were coming up in sessions where we were pitching customer and I kept hearing a similar sort of refrain. In essence what I tuned into was that there was a cohort of great value to an organisation that wasn't its employees and wasn't its customers. It was an amorphous group that had some connection to the organisation – a supplier, a stakeholder, a partner, an intermediary, a third party, a prospect, someone, anyone, with a common interest, who would find common cause with others under the aegis of a particular organisation. There it was, a clear gap...and I couldn't help myself. I did some quick mental visualisation and calculation – there was a bit of an app Venn Diagram thing going on, with a little bit of overlap functionally on one side with the colleague app, a little bit of overlap on the other with customer and then a new bold circle slap bang in the middle. The Engage Community app.

I've touched before on my deep-seated appreciation for my colleagues. They know me so well – and despite that, they are so forgiving! There are not that many CTOs who, having sweated blood for months developing a new customer app while simultaneously enhancing an existing colleague app, would be polite when faced with a CEO with a bit of an attention deficit disorder and a serial disregard for just what it would take to complete a holy trinity of engagement apps. Actually, Phil is not so much polite as phlegmatically resigned. He knows this is just how we are. As before with my customer epiphany, the acid test was, did he see it too? I asked the same question of John – was I properly onto something or was I just getting carried away with apps beginning with the letter C?

**Notes in the key of C**
Looking back, I can see that there were three 'mile markers' on this particular leg of the journey; three events that helped us shape and deliver the third C.

The first came out of discussions with a law firm looking at both internal and external engagement. We'd been talking to the marketing and comms team and I'd been struck by just how much amazing content they produced each week – not the digital chaff that makes for headache-inducing, ever-scrolling Twitter feeds, but valuable IP crafted by lawyers. I asked how they made their guidance notes and articles and thought pieces available to their key audiences – hosted on the website, circulated via email, signposted on social were the typical answers. My initial reaction? It felt limited, passive, fleeting, almost wasteful...when you had such content riches you really wanted them on maximum show, to be surfaced and shared and to have a proper shelf-life. They had to be actively distributed, made uber-accessible and kept in play – not atomised and lost in the social ether or buried on a website.

There was some ready acknowledgement in the room that it wasn't ideal – one of the firm's strategic aims was to become the go-to partner for the region's SMEs and much of their output and outreach was geared to this aim. But the traction and momentum wasn't where it should be: where there should have been a community, there was just one-way, one-time communication. There had to be a better way...

That was the catalyst. On the train home that night, I did that first bit of sketching out of what that 'better way' might look like. Initially it was oriented around content and its publication and distribution, the easiest and most obvious win. But as the Virgin train thundered back up north, I worked through a few other ideas and by the time we pulled into Manchester Piccadilly, I felt I had something. As a team we set to refining it, just as we had done with colleague and customer, working through each requirement and ticking off the technical capability to give us our final framework.

In this early iteration, the community app would help you:

- Digitally enable dynamic community building, 'in real life' (IRL) and virtual meet-ups and content sharing

- Cultivate social style communication, making it faster, easier, slicker to connect, chat and build relationships

- Amplify great content through the app, surfacing it to an invested audience and keeping it instantly accessible

- Encourage feedback, recognition, referrals, reward, ideation and loyalty, building stronger community bonds and encouraging members to make their own connections

- Supercharge experience and participation, lighting up events, hang-outs, networking, learning

- Segment your community members to deliver an ever more relevant and personalised experience

We had a few occasions where we were able to road-test these early thoughts and the reaction was wholly positive. And things started to crystallise further for me at the second 'mile marker': I started to understand more about why we were getting the reaction we were and that the opportunity was perhaps much, much bigger than I had originally conceived.

It started with an article I read on BBC News one weekend, highlighting an emerging trend of organisations pushing back from the Big Tech social platforms and opting instead for their own safe, flexible and engaging community spaces. The story told of how some of the big content players in YouTube were tiring of the constraints of the platform and its overlords and looking to build their own much smaller, but very engaged, committed communities online with their own dedicated platforms.

It was another example of people kicking against the thraldom of 'Big Tech', with consumers increasingly revaluating their relationships with social networks as they become more and more concerned with trolls, fake news, autonomous bots, data privacy issues, manipulative algorithms, scams and pervasively toxic environments.

This was a tide at work pushing the flow of positivity we enjoyed in the first flush of our community app play. As time went on, we were having the sort of conversations that would have been unimaginable a year previously, as everyone's default position back then was to leverage public social networks or established web forums. Now when we pitched the community app, we found ourselves talking to business leadership groups wanting a creative, collaborative space in which to talk more readily and freely; to carefully curate high value content; to offer practical support to members; and to strengthen existing relationships and nurture new ones.

The best conversations were with organisations who were already wrestling with the 'federating' requirement ie the need to bring together disparate third parties for a common purpose. These included a manufacturer wanting to support and link with its UK dealers more effectively; a health and social care provider bringing together service users, official bodies, medical specialists; a law firm looking to showcase its wealth of practice IP and foster closer connections between its lawyers, clients, prospects, introducers and advisors; the insurance company wanting to completely revitalise its broker network; and the retail organisation that has millions of customers every year - but minimal customer data available – that is taking the community 'special interest group' approach to tap into its diverse user base more effectively.

However, it wasn't just the desire for a fully-fledged community app that was driving these conversations – it was also the need to deploy one quickly and very cost-effectively. Sure, the techno whizzes cited in the BBC article may have been happy to invest a lot of time and money in their new channels, but in our long experience of boardroom IT conversations, the shorter the time to value, the better.

And here we could really deliver because, as we told the leadership sat in front of us, we'd done all the hard work for you – built the core app, with enough flex around branding and tooling to make it 'your app', alongside the other major upsides: an average deployment time of a month, and an average one-off cost of about half a skilled developer's annual salary. You'll recall Boris Johnson once saying that he had an oven-baked Brexit deal ready to go. Cue lots of obvious digs and 'half-baked' gags but as phrases go to sum up something all wrapped up and done...it was neat and I used it. Minus any attribution to BJ.

Warming to my theme, I would riff on the selling points...how you get all the best bits of social with none of the bad... enjoy full control with maximum functionality... privacy compliant... total visibility...a vehicle designed from the ground up for people and communities. The social posting functionality that we were encouraging in the colleague space? A perfect fit here too, with external audiences engaged and active on your platform – people with valid identities, first party data that you own and control, no longer at risk of Big Tech whim but instead free to power each other's social experience.

What's the saying? Big is beautiful? I argued regularly that the lustre of Big Tech seemed to be dimming in places and right on cue we had cosmetics firm Lush very publicly announcing that it was deactivating some of its social media accounts until the likes of Facebook/Meta "take action to provide a safer environment" for users.

I doubt Lush will be the last to quit. Every week we are talking to organisations open to an alternative for community creation and curation. There's no more defaulting to social networks by start-ups and seemingly less and less tolerance from established brands for what social media has become.

The public and commerce are sussing that while Big Tech appears to offer a free to use pass for community and relationship building, the truth is we are all paying a heavy price. Look up the phrase 'social media threat to democracy' and you'll see that concerns don't just stop at the level of individual harms and mental health impacts but go all the way up to existential risks to society and government and global security.

Suffice to say, the motivations to leave the thraldom of Meta et al are many and varied, major and minor. But the leavers are united in wanting to get to a nicer, kinder, richer, more honest and useful place – and the price you pay for that need only be a modest one.

So, goodbye Big Tech and hello small but perfectly formed community apps instead?

Seems that way from the projects I've seen in flight. And I've been wowed. Not by our app, but by our clients' imagination, innovation and inspiration when it comes to utilising the 'starter dough' of the app to make their respective community environments come alive. Everything is there, digital enablement, engagement, experience, empowerment, the resources, the tools, the collective spirit, the social vibe; and yet every community app is different, they've taken what we've offered and shaped it to the needs of both community owner and member.

Look at one of our very first projects in this space, the social enterprise, **vocL**; it perfectly reflects this undercurrent of a loss of trust in public platforms. When its launch made the national press, the message got some serious airtime. I've taken the liberty of quoting **vocL's** two founders as reported in The Times:

Juergen Maier CBE, Co-founder and Chair of vocL said, "Our platform enables invaluable access to otherwise inaccessible business leaders, communication experts, and journalists, to guide our mentees in mapping out unexplored areas of development, expanding their leadership skills, and strengthening their knowledge base. It is also a space where cross-company networking takes place, allowing people to connect with each other, debate matters, and bring important issues to light."

Henrietta Lindsell, Co-founder of vocL said, "vocL is a safe space where the next generation can talk with other, like-minded, business leaders from different generations about some of the most pressing issues facing business and society today".

"DO YOU THINK WE'RE TAKING THE 'SAFE SPACE' IDEA A BIT FAR?"

There you have it - an enabling safe space for talking, learning, sharing, debating, networking. Your space.

At times, the community app play has felt like the most electric and inventive of the three. Perhaps the more mature world of colleague and customer solutions just run on more constrained or conventional lines whereas community is young, it's only just starting on that whole 'art of the possible' exploration. But it starts from the strongest possible position – sitting on someone's home screen, an iconic doorway to your world.

**The wheels turn**

One of the reasons why I wanted to use the journey analogy for the book is that it gives me a very simple stylistic device to use to compensate for any narrative deficiencies! It helps signal that we have always had a forward momentum, energised at a very fundamental level by the 'art of the possible' and the science to make good change happen. As I hope I've conveyed, some of that is the consequence of my instinctively restless spirit, often pushing further and faster than others were ready for; but equally it comes from the team and clients, friends and associates, and from that social vortex that just throws out a steady stream of ideas and lightbulb moments.

And seemingly, from my letterbox at home.

Instances of our community app started to roll out during the second half of 2020, a new channel and connector for clients who, for all their enthusiasm for the freshly minted secure 'social buzz', were still looking at this through a commercial lens. And quite rightly. Everything we have ever done has been grounded in business imperatives – the need to improve, grow, invest, boost profits. Social media for business, community building, customer relationships, the digital enablement and potential for transformation that underpins every part of the Engage proposition, this stuff all has bottom-line impact.

The thing is, even before these early instances put down solid roots, I couldn't help but feel that there was more to community apps, some untapped potential, something I was missing. It was classic Wedgwood of course, that obsessive quest to just push for more, better, different...and I was annoyed with myself for not being able to see it. But as I fished in my letterbox one summer Saturday, I realised that sometimes you just need a helping hand to get that boulder up and over the hill.

In this instance, the helping hand took the form of a very classy and complex bit of cardboard packaging that was my new British Cycling (BC) membership pack.

Sadly, as I opened it at the breakfast table, the immediate aesthetic was slightly ruined by my marmalady dabs embellishing the matt laminate finish. But I pressed on, and inside I discovered a magazine, some leaflets, my new credit card sized plastic membership card, and on one of the gatefolds a very long alpha numeric 'friend get friend' referral code. In that moment, I was very content – cycling is my happy place and here were words and pictures aplenty to take me there.

It didn't last. I tried to remember when I had last received something through the post from BC. Last year's membership renewal. I thought about the contacts that I had with them between that point and this. A few email blasts. I wondered if I really wanted to put that membership card in my wallet. If I didn't, I would almost certainly lose it. Like I would the leaflet that told me what benefits and discounts were available to me. But they were both tinged with Frank Cooper's Original Oxford Course Cut so I wasn't keen. As for keeping that Mensa memory test of a code somewhere handy and safe...we're talking a household of three teenage children here, they can disappear the cat. There was a real risk of this whole package going in the recycling. What a waste – at every level.

And at that point, a synapse fired, the little wheels in my brain turned and I realised: what they really needed was an engagement platform and membership app. And the thing that had been missing that I'd been agonising over? A commanding commercial justification.

The 'me-sprinting-to-the-front-of-the-pack-and-then-dropping-back' cycling analogy I drew earlier? Here was a perfect example. And while I am – surprise – an enthusiastic backer of my ideas, life at Engage has always had more of the Chinese parliament about it than the benevolent dictatorship. People can have their say, they can challenge in an appropriate way, they can fly their own ideas – just as long as we reach a consensus that lets us keep moving forward with no backward recrimination.

Thus I went in on the Monday and gave the team my 'community-app-as-membership-app' thinking:

Membership organisations – the business networks and trade federations, the lifestyle, leisure and sporting associations, and the service-oriented, like roadside assistance and holiday clubs – they all face a common twin challenge: how to deliver the sort of membership value and experience that drives both retention and acquisition, while operating efficiently, profitably and sustainably.

Think of the community app but just repackaged. The draw for these organisations was a secure private app, oven-baked remember, sitting right there on a member's phone home screen. It could make them mobile-first at a stroke and provide the means to:

- Digitalise the membership experience end-to-end, from joining or renewing, to automatic alerts and digital membership cards, to buying or booking, to surveying and consulting

- Enable members to do more for themselves at their convenience, to connect more easily with other members and to contribute more actively and regularly

- Drive communication and engagement by flowing personalised content directly into a member's Facebook-style feed, reducing the reliance on the blunt instrument of generic emails

- Harness the viral power of a social network but within the safety of a private app, with members able to post, comment and share as individuals, with this informal 'socialcasting' style complementing more formal 'broadcasted' content.

- Improve the lean-ness and green-ness of back-end operations, reducing paper and postal costs and focusing more on agility and sustainability

The resultant discussion wouldn't have troubled Hansard if we were putting it on parliamentary record – agreement was instant and unanimous. It was a 'go'.

## Conscious uncoupling

The 'community app for membership organisations' – to be hereafter referred to as the membership app for clarity – was immediately positioned as a modernising force, offering a win-win: new levels of enablement, experience, engagement, convenience and overall member value on the one hand; and on the other the chance to be leaner and greener, slicker and smarter at the back-end.

In keeping with our journey ethos, it doesn't have to be all or nothing, or at least not all at once. We've always been acutely aware that whether you are dealing with a workforce or an external audience, you have a broad demographic in play. Not everyone is a digital native wedded to their phone; some people like to receive hard copies of magazines; others want to flash their card rather than faff around with Face ID. The app is your analogue world made digital for those who want to go there; it's an option, an extra layer, something to transition to slowly, quickly, whatever you prefer.

Our initial soundings confirmed we were right to be sensitive: digital transformation is an aspiration for many but there needs to be a throttle to pace the journey. We can't impose or enforce, only encourage and facilitate. But we're committed and going all-in because this is too compelling a use case. If we use the same turnover metric to define our target market here as we have with all our industry sectors - £10m+ – then you're looking at over 4000 organisations. A good proportion will be playing catch up – we want to help them overtake.

Because the Community C is often quoted third in line, I'm sometimes asked if it was just an afterthought or whether it's the poor relation to its colleague and customer siblings. Categorically not. In fact, rather ironically, it is the app that has been on the longest, most exciting journey. It's a bit like those trains that are formed of eight coaches, where the train arrives at Station X and is uncoupled in the middle, with the first four coaches forming one train to head off to Station Y and the rear four coaches forming another for Station Z. It's still the same train in essence, but the two parts are destined for different things. On the one line we have the community app as originally conceived, a networking play with its social and relationship vibe to the fore; on the other line, now uncoupled and pulling away and getting up its own head of steam is that app reimagined for membership organisations.

Either way, our third C and engagement family member was firmly on track.

**THE SIGNAL FOR CONTENT**

**CHAPTER 8**

They know what they're about, those packaging design wizards....so many unplanned purchases made because of the allure of the outer product look, rather than any appreciation of what's inside. But it was this container/contents relationship that gave me a revelatory 'penny drop' moment. That and bunny ears.

08

The wisdom went something like this: when we set clients up with their app we are just giving them a container, and in its shiny UX there is that same attraction to the 'wrapper'. It looks cool, sophisticated, intriguing, you want to pick it up and do the digital equivalent of turning it over, feeling the quality, admiring the design, the structure, the cleverness of the construct. But the app for all its aesthetics is still just the outer skin, just the container. It's what is inside that really counts. The outside might get the instant reaction, the immediate wow; but it's the inside that must deliver the enduring value, the consistent returns, a reason to commit.

And now for the bunny ears. It was a Snapchat filter, I looked ridiculous (thanks, kids) but I was also struck by the cleverness of the tech, and the ability of the social media companies to always be switching up their offer, by innovating within their apps so you could innovate in turn with your content. I started to notice other creative output that fell into this tech-enabled or platform-dependent category - augmented reality videos, personalised pieces, content that was obviously sat as part of a workflow, all items that were drawing on the native functionality within a platform rather than simply being published through it. I mentioned my British Cycling membership earlier...what price a branded, personalised digital membership card with a QR code for discounts and embedded referral rewards?

That realisation excited me because here was another differentiator. Yes, we absolutely understood that the real engagement magic lies in the content you pour into your app. But there are a lot of digital content providers out there, specialists in their field and what would we have to gain by competing with them? Far better surely to carry on with our fundamental levelling-up mission - making business tech like consumer tech – and take a leaf out of the social media giants' book: focus on platform-enabled content, use the cleverness of the tech to elevate the content. By innovating in this way we could help clients deliver output that was far more immersive, experiential, memorable, and engaging. No-one was doing this, indeed we realised that no-one could do this as they had neither the delivery platform nor the deep engagement IP. All we needed was the content creation capability and...oh look, we already had that in-house!

Admittedly, its focus was our own marketing and bringing the apps' UX alive through branding and custom design, as well as undertaking R&D for future app developments around augmented reality; we'd even built a high-end greenscreen facility and production suite on the lower ground floor to underline our intent. Could we not use all these factors to produce content that lives within and is enabled via our platform?

I liked the idea because we wanted to have some skin in the content game – but it had to be enshrined in the tech. So, a one-off video for someone? Not our bag. An AR-based training program served through the app? A health and well-being module leveraging alerts, calendars and personal preferences? No problem, please take a seat. This approach gave us clarity and direction and a point of difference; and since it was taken we've had a huge amount of fun exploiting the creative potential that lives within our tech and delivering content that is brought to life via the Engage platform.

It also helps us negotiate the wider content question with confidence and authority. We know full well it is content that delights, excites, and engages, and has users coming back for more. Findings from our early analysis of why previous employee engagement projects had a habit of petering out had highlighted this particularly: the inability to consistently put out enough content, or at least enough interesting or relevant content. Project owners would start off 'all guns blazing', burning through their launch plan and the content they'd dammed up in preparation...transitioning from flood to drip to drop to nothing.

You can see why it happens. In the external engagement world, there is typically very generous provision for marketing and promotion, with much of the work entrusted to dedicated creative agencies. Internal engagement can't always rely on the same.  Not every company has internal comms professionals working for them; if they do, the app brings in a whole new area of editorial responsibility and ups the demands for output, putting further pressure on probably limited resources. That goes double, treble, quadruple for busy HRs - who may have the people gene but not necessarily the creative marker to be able to pull off the content trick.

So what's an app devoid of any decent content worth? Not much! And are you going to achieve engagement success with a worthless app? No, and that's precisely why I have become very bold in the boardrooms of clients and prospects, opining that if they don't have a content strategy in place then their engagement project will falter then fail.

As I noted earlier, we've already provided plenty of platform-powered content, which has happily blended with the 'straight' digital output of videos, podcasts, blogs, photo streams etc. And you have to look to the bigger prize here - good content, of all types, translating into higher consumption, generating the sort of consistent usage that reinforces the success credentials of the app.

## Three become four

We duly made content our fourth C but with a very clear purview. This was never about us owning the content piece, or removing the burden entirely from clients, especially those focused on colleague programmes. For a start, content has to be owned internally. Yes, we can share our learning, suggest initiatives, leverage the native functionality - but we cannot be you! It's you, the client, that knows your people, your organisation, your backstory; it's you that is fully cognisant of prevailing attitudes and latent sensitivities, the demographic challenges and influential cliques; it's you taking the temperature of the organisation, making the sort of calls and judgments you can never do as an outsider. But we can stand with you, advise and assist, and it has served up another angle for me to go at in helping HR and IC voices to get heard in the boardroom.

In January 1996, Bill Gates wrote an essay titled 'Content is King'. His basic hypothesis was that content was where the real money would be made on the Internet, just as it was in broadcasting. He wasn't wrong, was he? At the end of every internet connection then and every app now is a human being wanting to be entertained, informed, involved, enthused, reassured, inspired. Perhaps the commercial models didn't quite go the way he thought they would, but no matter, we are all avid consumers of content.

The beauty of the 'Content is King' phrase is in its brevity - it lands instantly. And in our world it helps position content not as an afterthought, not as secondary to its container, but as the absolute prime consideration. And that is what gives me the confidence to say to people: if you haven't got a content strategy then your engagement strategy will fail.

## Content as a service

But that's not the whole content story. Early positive adoption of an app by a user base is critical; and the creative talent we have, grounded in engagement excellence, plays an integral role in that process. It provides support in crucial areas including:

### App design and build

Giving you the strongest branding and slickest look and feel alongside total functional alignment.

### App launch and promotion

Starting your engagement efforts at the earliest possible opportunity, reaching out with a communications campaign to build awareness, generate excitement, overcome change barriers, and drive positive adoption on go-live.

### Strategic and advisory

Regularly evaluating what's working from a content perspective, a user experience perspective and a business outcomes perspective, to inform content direction, minor app design tweaks and major refresh projects.

**Content-ed**

Looking back now, I think the content 'C' was quite a brave move – for a technology-led business – but one that has certainly differentiated us and added considerable value.

If I'm asked what it is that makes ESG especially compelling, then I'd be tempted to highlight the following:

- We have hundreds of successful app projects behind us, built on diligent design work and persuasive, comprehensive launch efforts

- We know exactly how to design and deliver the best in platform-enabled content, drawing on advanced skills like AR to really supercharge the user experience

- We're immersed in engagement every day, so we can bring that domain expertise in to help you make the right content calls

I'll confess too that at a personal level, I'm all over this!

The teenage geeky Phil who loved new, shiny tech is still very present in the adult Mr Digital and he keeps the tech fires burning.

"YOU'VE EITHER GOT A SECRET LIFE
OR YOU'VE BEEN USING THAT GREEN SCREEN AGAIN!"

I think he's there in all our AR output for starters. I remember when iPhones first offered native support for AR – I couldn't order one quick enough as I just had to start tinkering and I've followed their evolution ever since. Today the LiDAR sensors available on the latest iPhones are opening up a new world of immersive experiences and I want our embedded content offering to continually reflect what is achievable, and to push the creative envelope where we can – as long as it supports the engagement strategy. And that's where we are at – always looking to get the most out of the available tech, knowing how to make it really sing and pumping it full of cracking tunes that hit the engagement top notes.

THE ENGAGEMENT ENGINE

## CHAPTER 9

I am very fond of Manchester. I have lived there for over twenty years and it is, coincidentally, widely regarded as the home of my two great passions, computing and cycling. All three worlds regularly collide on my regular group rideouts through and around Greater Manchester and Cheshire, with work and business always being the top topic for saddle chat and pub banter. Last summer I was out one Sunday and I just happened to mention a Destination Engage event we'd held in the week as I was still buzzing from it.

It had been the first time we'd had this particular client's entire C team with us in the office; they'd been live on the employee side for about 18 months and were making encouraging noises about their engagement journey so we'd facilitated a Destination Engage event for them.

My very good friend Mike who was riding alongside turned to me and asked: "How do you get a whole exec team to schlep up to Manchester and spend the day listening to you?" None taken, mate.

It might have been the lure of a private dinner and overnight stay in the stunning Hotel Gotham just around the corner from the office; or the fun and games we had in the studio with the cameras and silly AR filters; or even the pizza and prosecco party we had on the roof terrace as a last hurrah. But more probably it was because of all the efforts we have made over the years to educate the C suite or leadership team on the value of engagement. Our single biggest challenge has been to elevate engagement to a board level conversation. We've ridden that challenge all the way to this point, on the way giving HR a proper voice at the table and getting colleague engagement validated as the bedrock, the logical foundation stone for your end-to-end engagement journey.

Which brings me neatly back to my railway analogy...

You already know how this story ends, with us drawing up to Destination Engage via Platform 5C – colleague, community and customer apps, content, and consulting.

So we have the train (the platform-based tech) and the electric supply (the content) – which just leaves the driver, right?

For a long while we never thought about consulting per se, in as much as we never separated it out, never referred to it as such. That type of work? It was just this thing we did. We thought it a natural part of the sales process to sit down with a prospect and undertake a diligent, searching discovery process; so that we could all understand and agree on the problems, highlight the opportunities and illustrate what success would look like in properly quantifiable terms, not some loose generic benefits. A business case is often many hours in the making and when they are presented, they impress with their situational grasp and granular evidence.

Equally, when onboarding a new client, we have real, named, accessible people on hand throughout. And those friendly, knowledgeable humans hand over to equally friendly, knowledgeable humans who are charged with helping our clients drive and maintain engagement success – they advise, they cajole, they keep them honest, always referencing the project back to its initial success criteria and relating progress to key milestones.

In short, there is a lot of handholding, a lot of knowhow sharing, a lot of pragmatic help – which is in stark contrast to the majority of our app competitors who are happy to disintermediate the whole human element completely. All rather ironic given that engagement is a people thing. But the standard approach appears to be to throw out the twin lifelines of an online knowledge base and a bot-led support desk. And yet the idea that every issue or concern in such a complex, nuanced, textured subject can find its rightful answer or reassuring reply in a data repository is ridiculous — but then zero human touch has its obvious fiscal upside for the vendor.

Sure, we give our clients access to a knowledge base and a support desk, but that's where we start, not end. Clients have all that human intelligence and interaction as an overlay; our engagement success team (our project and account managers) do their job by properly engaging.

Though we came to realise that this was quite a differentiator (it has been cited many times as the reason why we get the nod) we still didn't rush to assume the mantle of 'consultants'. The engagement success team was and is very much focused on the project deliverables initially and then they segue into more of a tactical account management operation.

But as we started to look at engagement in the round, this potential to pivot from internal to external, and developing the associated community and customer apps, we realised that it wasn't just enough for us to go out there with our uber-enthusiasm for some new tech we'd dreamed up. We had to be able to talk strategy, to articulate precisely the rationale for the pivot. Obviously, with the hard yards behind us on the colleague side, we already had a strong strategic grasp of the internal dynamics. But externally, we needed to do our homework and it was this realisation I think that was the real prompt for the CXO-level peering push we started to make. The Engage top team needed to be out there talking to the CEOs and their chief operating officers, chief marketing officers, finance heads, IT directors...if engagement in the round was to fly, we couldn't just be this little square peg in our little square HR hole.

Our first job, though, was to be clear on what we had to offer each member of the executive group. While I was personally keen to talk to the CEO, as the person responsible for orchestrating everything, we had to be comfortable entering the domain of every CXO. We had to give them something worthy of further thought, something that they could take back to their own departments for them to get excited about too. We felt comfortable answering the 'why for the organisational buyer' – that was all enshrined in the business case – but we knew we had to nail the 'why for the individual buyer' just as much. We needed everyone to feel like they had skin in the game, and some of the time it was about tapping into a particular person's psychology – were they risk-averse? Did they want to be a hero? Were they an innovator? Were they really focused on delivering their plan?

**Something for everyone**
But for a lot of the time too it was simply setting out the benefits very clearly of something they might not have been that familiar with. Engagement as we see it, grounded in digital enablement and relevant across the whole enterprise, is not yet a well-worn chapter in the business playbook. That's why we've spent time carefully considering the 'what's in it for me' question: CXOs convinced on an individual level will be stronger advocates for programs pitched at an organisational level.

If I had an exec team in that fabled elevator for 30 seconds, then I would encourage each one to view our end-to-end engagement solution in the following terms:

*All* - An offering engineered to deliver right across the C suite. For one thing, it helps create a great people strategy, an ambition that should be shared by everyone around the boardroom table, not just by HR. For another, it offers up real value for the individual CXO, simultaneously solving different problems for different people - and offering plenty of scope to change, improve, and innovate too.

*Chief People Officer* - A comprehensive culture-changing toolkit that gets to work out-of-the-box in connecting the centre to the edge, and giving every employee the information, support, resources and respect needed to boost satisfaction, loyalty, wellness, performance and productivity.

*Chief Operations Officer* - A platform that can be embedded into the operational fabric to drive up efficiency, safety and quality, and light up change initiatives such as net zero targets or underpin process improvement programs.

*Chief Information Officer* - An adaptive overlay that unlocks mobility, kicks out shadow IT, reinforces data compliance, and aggregates your point solutions, with ready to go APIs and single sign-on, letting you build out extended colleague or customer digital environments.

*Chief Marketing Officer* - An alternative marketing, customer service and business development engine, the chance to properly own the customer lifecycle, to nurture relationships continuously, to channel and amplify great content directly; and to provide a quality experience consistently.

*Chief Financial Officer* - A tech investment that just keeps giving: in the water quickly and driving that bottom-line improvement, through increased productivity, improved customer retention, increased customer spend, less waste, lower staff attrition, reduced sickness, fewer accidents, reduced operational, fiscal and reputational risk.

*Chief Executive Officer* - Everything you need to build and sustain a mobile-first, digitally-enabled world where passion for your customers, colleagues and communities can enrich people, accelerate progress, and supercharge revenues.

Okay, I'll grant you that I would have had to deliver that elevator pitch at machine-gun speed to be within my 30 seconds, but you get the idea – these are the respective prisms we urge every CXO to look through along with the broader organisational view.

That messaging gave us a positive start. It certainly gelled and we started to pull together plenty of affirmatory detail into each CXO pitch to lend weight to the overall pitch, particularly those occasions where there was an obvious end-to-end opportunity. But we also weren't kidding ourselves: we are execs ourselves, we know how many strategic, financial and operational balls have to be juggled, how intricate and political corporate fabrics can be, how difficult it is to penetrate full brains and busy lives to just insert a germ of an idea.

There's that famous Thomas Edison quote - "Genius is one percent inspiration and 99 percent perspiration." I have no claims to genius but... the C suite push was a good idea and the competitive cyclist in me was no stranger to determination and perseverance, so it was very much game on. We had to keep on at the boardroom.

**"IT'S THE NEW ELEVATOR PITCH FOR THE COVID ERA.
WHAT COULD POSSIBLY GO WRONG?"**

What helped immeasurably was that we were all signed up to this idea of the engagement journey; and the more we developed our thinking, the more conversations we had with prospects, the more solidly it took shape. Just like every 'engine driver' learning their route, we became much more familiar with everything on the map and much more assured about how to apply the power for a smooth ride.

Today we are at a level where we know exactly what's necessary to get started, to get traction, to get to the next stage and ultimately to get to the end – and it's under the banner of the 'consulting C' that we are doing our utmost to share that experience and learning.

We've taken every possible step. For example, Hubspot is one of the world's leading CRM systems, and if we wanted to fully realise our vision of a CRM-enabled customer app then we needed to immerse ourselves in all things Hubspot. That was best done by becoming a partner – a status usually reserved for digital marketing agencies but we were duly appointed, the UK's first Hubspot integration partner drawn from the technology sector.

At a stroke, chief marketing officers now have access to a full solution, not a partial one, as we can deliver a customer strategy predicated on CRM, powered by the Hubspot back end, delivered through the Engage customer app, and brought to life through our content.

We haven't just looked outwards for inspiration but internally too. All that IP and practical wisdom we were gaining? All the consulting value we were accruing, even if we were shy of calling it that? Maybe now was the time to focus and fashion something substantive and practical for the C suite.

Our first output was the Engagement Maturity Curve (EMC). Given that engagement is a journey we wanted to help organisations orient themselves more easily as to their present position. It's based on a matrix of engagement disciplines and the performance or 'maturity' in each; so not just useful for situational awareness but also for highlighting where the effort needs to be focused to get further along the curve.

The EMC inevitably triggered more deep-dive conversations, and that was the prompt for developing our own Gartner-inspired interactive tool, the CEO Navigator. The Navigator has two primary functions: to get some of that knowledge transfer going on at board level; and to facilitate conversations and collaboration around strategy.

It draws on all the lived knowhow, the data and analytics, the sector knowledge, the war stories, everything that we have in our locker that can be taken wholesale or cherry-picked and synthesised with the ambitions or challenges of the company in front of us. It's framed in such a way that it mirrors our 'mapping the journey' approach. You can take it at your own pace; there's a starting point, an end point, plenty of request stops and milestones en route. But this way you get to review the whole engagement proposition fully in context: to see the logical progression; to appreciate the considerations enterprise-wide; to understand the inputs, outputs and outcomes; to know what questions to ask and decisions to take; and ultimately to value the 5Cs approach in terms of securing engagement success.

In my own CEO-to-CEO peering sessions, I like to fire up the Navigator as it's a brilliant way of focusing all our minds on not so much how far we've come but on where the next opportunities lie and how best to plan for them. It brings clarity and spurs proper consideration and honest evaluation – more than anything it keeps engagement alive in the boardroom and owned by the board.

Boards need evidence of success too, of course. We can't be planning for the future if we've been falling short on the business case. But they also need to have a sense of what good looks like. We wanted to help organisations more easily measure and benchmark their performance, so we developed another interactive tool, the Engagement Index. It lets users assess how they stand in comparison to a sector baseline and lets them home in on a whole range of short, medium and long-term tactics to improve their engagement metrics. It helps that we have vast quantities of anonymised data across multiple sectors to draw on, and all that close quarters, day-to-day advisory experience to weave in to maximise the IP within the Index.

You would have thought that regular exec reviews and a clutch of clever consulting tools would be enough for me, wouldn't you? Plenty there to allow me to have those board-level sessions I crave...but even empowered thus, I still wanted something more. By now you'll know that I'm just wired that way, restlessly obsessing about how far we can take things. If we're back on the analogy, I think this was the moment of getting up a full head of steam on the engagement express, in search of that ultimate 'peak engagement' sweetspot.

Which is precisely how I ended up that day, down in the studio, with that CEO, the F word and a dreadful sense of foreboding.

When I look at the Destination Engage concept now, from the safety of my current position with several very successful events under our belts and all foreboding dissipated, I'm really happy that we made the call and invested so much of ourselves into it. We didn't have to, we could have kept the consulting sell conventional, the technical demos classical, all conference rooms and Powerpoints.

But curating these bespoke events, which have seen us brainstorm on the roof, build augmented reality worlds in our studio, banter on the oche at Flight Club, bring new strategies into being by the end of that evening's tasting menu, and so much more, all of this is the perfect distillation of everything we do, every part of the journey, and more than that, it's a reflection of every part of us. We take what we do very seriously, but it doesn't mean that we have to take ourselves too seriously. That paradox is perfectly encapsulated by Destination Engage.

Where it gets its real motive power from is that there's engagement at the atomic heart of the event itself: it brings people together to connect, interact, share, listen and learn. It's creative, relaxed, enjoyable, but packed with potential to reshape every facet of engagement - colleague, customer and community – and energise every part of the enterprise. CXO-level guests tend to come with problems they need to work through and leave with plans they want to work on. And that's all we ever wanted to achieve really – to have engagement better understood, properly appreciated and enthusiastically championed across the C suite. With Destination Engage, engagement has finally arrived in the boardroom.

## ALL CHANGE

### CHAPTER 10

A rather remarkable occurrence happened at the beginning of the year: Apple hit the $3 trillion dollar valuation mark briefly during the day's trading, powered in large part by the continued dominance of the iPhone. That's more than the annual GDP of the UK. And we invented the wretched thing! Well, young inventor Alexander Graham Bell did back in 1876, and I'm sure he would marvel at the telephonic progeny his patent would ultimately spawn.

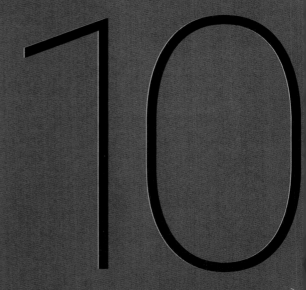

I'm rather in awe too, as those sort of figures (they're not far off Germany's GDP either, just for more context) do really bring it home to you how transformational the iPhone revolution has been; how far it has reached, how far it has impacted, and how fast and completely it has changed so many things in our day to day lives.

In fact, I'm not sure the word 'transformation' does it justice, because what Apple – and the Androiders - has done is little short of epoch-defining. So much power in every person's pocket...I can remember a road trip I made in the States in the late 90s. We had maps, a Rough Guide and an encyclopaedic knowledge of motel chain logos, the illuminated versions of which we would keep an eagle eye out for as we cruised down the freeway in search of a bed for the night. We used phones boxes to call home. Our plane tickets had carbon papers in them. Now when I'm on holiday my phone is as critical as my passport and the realisation that you've forgotten your charging cable has you cursing as you hare off to buy your 45th one that year.

Likewise, when I'm at work or at play, the phone is my constant companion. I don't need to miss anything or anyone. And it's the same for hundreds of millions of people, billions in fact. Which is why Apple is counting its trillions. And it's why I have always championed mobile-first strategies – from well before the iPhone era. At the beginning of the book, I talked about my time at Rekoop; my colleague Phil and I, and the team we had, revolutionised how the legal sector recorded its time technically, and altered how they thought about it too.

The game-changer was mobile – as fee earners enjoyed the emancipation afforded them by their new Blackberry and laptop, they needed something that would keep pace with their need to record and capture time accurately and promptly. Time recording on the mobile rapidly became the default, lawyers who had always detested and resisted filling in timesheets became if not exactly evangelistic then at least cooperative, and the hygiene of time data – in terms of accuracy and completeness and speed of submission – was taken to a whole new level.

But let's be clear. The technology was just the enabler; it was the thinking we wrapped around it that did the true transforming. We challenged law firms on how they thought about and utilised these accurate time data sets, and gave them the means to move beyond simplistic time and billing behaviour. For example, we encouraged a far more sophisticated analysis of the 'cost of production' ie how and where lawyers were spending their time. The resultant insights allowed law firms for the first time to get a real grip on pricing and to respond confidently to growing client demands for alternative billing arrangements – when you know what it costs you, you know what to sell it for.

In similar vein, we brought in the real-time tracking of fees against matter progress, which helped give the then nascent legal project management discipline some teeth and credibility, because they had what were essential performance metrics at their fingertips. The new levels of visibility, traceability and granularity when it came to time recorded also revealed the reckless and unwitting level of discounting and write-offs that went on; that went to the very heart of the business and was taken straight to the leadership table.

The transformation opportunities kept coming – with enough 'production data' banked, could law firms now look at mirroring the behaviours of 'big business' and study things like resource utilisation, capacity planning, client centricity, service commoditisation, delivery models etc? Looking back, it wasn't enough for us just to be the incidental enablers of data flow - we wanted to transform how firms thought about it, leveraged it, and optimised it so they could in turn transform their own businesses.

Today with my Engage hat on, there are just so many echoes of that journey. Here we are again advocating a mobile-first strategy because engagement is built on connectivity and phones create an invisible web between us all. (I say phone, you and I know it's a portable personal computer in exquisitely miniaturised form but phone is a lot easier to say). As before, this ubiquitous, universal connection of people and entities is not transformative of itself, it is purely enabling. To kick on from enablement to true digital transformation, one also has to work out how best to effect change rather than just supply the technical change agent.

In legal, that combination of tech and IP modernised an archaic approach, recasting 'administrative' time and billing as something altogether more dynamic, powerful and grown-up, garnering attention from the top table. Now here we are again with the 5Cs - fusing the 'tech to enable' with the 'thinking to transform' and solving the conundrum of how to engage with key audiences easily, effectively and cost-efficiently. And if you need a reminder why that matters, it's just a simple equation: the more you engage people, the better able you are to deliver positive outcomes.

The 5Cs formula has helped us substantiate the idea of enterprise engagement and made us comfortable using the solution word and platform styling; it's opened doors to the boardroom too.

And based on our conversations there, I do feel that we're at an inflection point.

Hitherto most organisations have tended to break engagement down into discrete tasks and commodity tools: the purchase and deployment of a colleague app, a customer app, a community app, maybe a mobile intranet app, a messaging app, whatever. They may be one offs, or they may be part of a grand plan – and that's fine because down the line, if they want to take a next step, we can have that discussion, map out the journey, get them to the next destination. That's the whole rationale of the 5Cs. It's a self-paced success route.

But I'm seeing signs that some organisations are looking for...how I should put this...a non-stopping service? So those conversations in the boardroom...there's little reference to the words 'app' or 'tool' for starters. They're orbiting instead around the concept of enterprise engagement - that amalgam of engagement platform and engagement IP.

So no more looking through the separate or even sequential prisms of colleague, customer and community engagement; it's a single prism now, it's just engagement. And this more singular lens is producing some interesting results. It seems to me that freed from siloed project thinking/doing, people are coming at it much more holistically, more freely, more innovatively, with bolder plans that can stretch across whole constituencies – colleagues, customers, suppliers, third parties, prospects, embracing them all rather than entertaining each one. When you come at it this way the possibilities seem limitless, the applications infinite, whether it's solving big problems, or exploiting new opportunities.

For instance. In front of me right now are strategic plans for two clients who have taken the 'express' route: they've bought into engagement, they're excited about its potential, they've thought deeply about it. You can almost see this golden thread of engagement being weaved through the business from back to the front, top to the bottom and then out to that wider constituency, looping in everyone. And the pot of gold at the end of the engagement rainbow? The opportunity not just to revolutionise their business but to change the way a whole industry does business.

Both clients see these plans sat squarely under the aegis of digital transformation. Wow, to think that engagement – once memorably dismissed by a CEO as 'HR fluff' – is now being seen in this light, with the potential to challenge orthodoxies and reshape whole sectors. It's galvanising and electrifying, and as to how much it can achieve and influence, who knows. But rest assured that Mr Digital and friends will be along for the ride.

## THE TRAIN NOW ARRIVING

### CHAPTER 11

We may have ended up at Destination Engage but that's not really where I want your thoughts to dwell. Think instead about the 5Cs-driven engagement journey that we've been on – and treat this end point as your starting point.

11

And while this has been the narrative of the 5Cs, this final chapter finds us in the orbit of another C. Unseen, unknown and unplanned for – until Easter 2020. There has been so much written about Covid that I would do anything not to give it more airtime, but it has changed things for us – a positive shunt, not a derailment, so it's all good. How far and how quickly we return to our previous ways, we'll have to wait and see. If I've learnt anything from the pandemic, it's that predictions are not really that good a guide to actuals and that human behaviour has a remarkable propensity to confound every expectation. Let's not waste time on conjecture but focus on fact.

First, you need to remember that we were serving up solutions to naturally distributed, non-desked organisations long before viral vectors steered us homewards. We were also supporting traditional desked corporates in their bid to refresh internal systems like intranets. Many companies were wrestling more broadly with digital transformation and modernisation projects; indeed, most of our app deployments were coming under that umbrella. But my word, the sales cycle could be an agonisingly slow process at times - ponderous, protracted and full of barriers and 'nos' and 'sorrys' and reductive arguments against blatant good sense ideas. Here you are in one breath saying you want to move on, and in the next you are refusing to budge.

Then came Covid, Boris at his lectern and a whole new lexicon of lockdowns, social distancing, WFH, and the treble-jabbed. They say that necessity is the mother of invention; well, judging from what happened next, it is also the mother of motivation, perspiration, and all-hands-to-the-pump action too. The fact is, the world of work sorted itself out almost overnight.

Key workers – almost all of whom fell into that distributed workforce category – are adaptive by default and rose magnificently to the challenge, superheroes all, masked but no capes, sporting garb from white coats to hi-viz jackets, hairnets to helmets. The white-collar corporate world may have become more mobile and more digital in the last decade but that could not have readied them for the 'Closed' sign being hung on cities and towns up and down the land. And yet with days and weeks, they were functioning and to pretty high levels too. I remember calling my bank and having a great chat with a lady called Lisa who was sat in her living room in Coventry. Did it matter? Not a jot. Her world was at her fingertips even while her cat was on her lap.

In the months that followed, I read story after story about firms' speed of response, which segued into more reflective commentaries about how they'd been able to do it and how their success in doing it had completely changed outlooks and attitudes. I think this seminal change was best summed up by an IT director of a professional services firm who said that they had achieved in six weeks what it would have taken six years to do in normal circumstances. Perhaps a slight exaggeration for effect but you get the point: if vaccines were our shot in the arm for a healthier future, the pandemic was the defibrillator that shocked UK plc into action.

We saw it ourselves immediately. As you can imagine, a mobile-first, communications-led app was the 'must-have' accessory of the season. We got the calls and now there was no option for companies to mull it over, consult widely, benchmark it, trial it, or any of those can-kicking-down-the-road behaviours. They just signed and we just rolled it out. In one case, we had 10,000 users live within five days of contract signature.

And you know what? Their worlds, previously so hidebound and risk-averse, didn't cave in or collapse with this unseemly haste and enforced subversion of corporate norms. In fact, amazing things happened, the Lisas of Coventry happened, all the world kept turning. Today we are seeing the enduring upside of that era: when we go into see people now, there isn't the fear of change or hesitancy to innovate that we used to encounter. From what has been hopefully a once-in-a-lifetime event, they've had an unexpected dabble with the 'art of the possible'; and they love what they saw, what they achieved and now they want more. They're confident, purposeful, planning for what's next on the digital agenda. Enablement, experience and engagement are very much to the fore, and that's impacting us directly: conversations are happening far more readily, engagement strategies are being mapped out more fully, and most telling of all, project sponsorship is coming from the board from the absolute get-go. That is a huge change. From the C we didn't see coming.

## Funny turn

It's funny how life turns out. The seed for everything Engage was this desire to enhance business through digital technology; and to do so by enabling those in the workplace to enjoy the same rich, engaging and immersive experience as they did at the breakfast table or on the sofa. As I mentioned at the beginning, for years now consumer tech has massively outpaced business tech and we wanted to leverage all of it – social, messaging, self-service, mobile intranet, this whole on-demand, real-time world. And we created highly functional but also very cool apps as a result. With Covid and the WFH movement, all of a sudden those cool apps were being used at the breakfast table and on the sofa that had in so many ways been their original inspiration.

We were also cognisant of a shifting landscape. A research study released late in 2021 reported that three fifths of workers were planning to switch jobs as a result of Covid. Then there's the continuing narrative around labour shortages, skills gaps, and growing worker entitlement in terms of how and where they work. Internally things are running hot so HRs and their CXO allies need to more alive than ever to anything that shifts the staff attraction and retention needle. Does engagement have a role to play in that? Dur, was JVT the coolest guy on the Covid planet? Of course it does.

The big question is just how far you can take it and how much you can achieve. I know someone who might be able to help with that.

Back to that positive shunt I mentioned earlier. We've felt that all the way through to external engagement too. The 'art of the possible' is a vast canvas and buoyed by their achievements during Covid, organisations are wanting to have that end-to-end or more rounded, 360° engagement conversation earlier and to see what sort of a future they can paint for their customers and/or wider communities of interest. The prolonged disruption to 'normal service', the enforced separation and universal dispersal that went on, these have all prompted a bit of a rethink seemingly. It's maybe not enough just to get back to doing what you were doing before; societal habits and consumer expectations and individual behaviours have changed, and it feels like we need to change too, to respond in kind. Perhaps now is the time to remake relationships and reshape businesses.

We have a great example of that going on right now, and proof if proof were needed that engagement, and our take on it, is firmly enterprise grade, and the stuff of board level conversations. We're currently working with a major insurance group, a top 20 global player with a network of 700 UK brokers; each of those brokers has a policyholder base running into the tens and hundreds of thousands.

Our initial project in early 2021 was to deliver a community app that would connect the insurer to their brokers, providing a variety of business resources and sales support to drive mutual success. We undertook a second project very soon after to roll out a colleague app to bring together the insurer's thousand-strong global workforce. And within another three months, we were having a conversation about enabling every broker to roll out their own customer app (which basically just required a deft repurposing of the existing community app) to usher in a whole new level of end user experience. Here was a priceless opportunity to redefine every relationship and lock in the loyalty that comes from true lifecycle management. All up, that's zero to a potential 1m+ users on an Engage-powered platform in less than nine months – as an example of end-to-end engagement, I'm not sure I will find better. So, a fairly big shunt on reflection.

Throughout the book I've used the word 'social' a lot. Please don't misconstrue that as somehow lightweight, that we're just dealing with digital ephemera. Our desire to bring some equality to the tech experience led us to borrow heavily from the Big Tech players, yes – but we've brought all their good stuff into a secure, private space. Your space, your rules, compliant by design, connective by default. It's the best of social, but for business, and it is full of opportunity and potential. We haven't even scratched the surface yet.

One final word. The train that's making its engagement journey...it's picking up passengers all the time, employees, third parties, suppliers, stakeholders, customers, clients, prospects, influencers. These people, they are all agents of growth, profit and success. Treat them well, support the individual, nurture the collective, own their lifecycle, enable, empower and engage them as much as you can, and you will win. And if you win, we all win.

I think the customary words are now 'The End'. But I hope for many of you out there it will also be 'The Beginning'.

PS. Thanks, dad!

Printed in Great Britain
by Amazon

82033684R00085